T0278326

Teilhard de Chardin

A Book of Hours

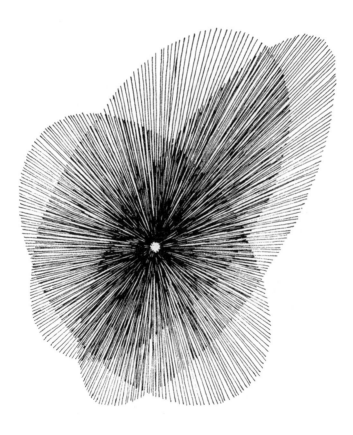

Teilhard de Chardin

A Book of Hours

Edited by
Kathleen Deignan, CND
and
Libby Osgood, CND

ORBIS BOOKS
Maryknoll, New York 10545

Second Printing, March 2024

Founded in 1970, Orbis Books endeavors to publish works that enlighten the mind, nourish the spirit, and challenge the conscience. The publishing arm of the Maryknoll Fathers and Brothers, Orbis seeks to explore the global dimensions of the Christian faith and mission, to invite dialogue with diverse cultures and religious traditions, and to serve the cause of reconciliation and peace. The books published reflect the views of their authors and do not represent the official position of the Maryknoll Society. To learn more about Maryknoll and Orbis Books, please visit our website at www. orbisbooks.com.

Manufactured in the United States of America

Library of Congress Cataloging-in-Publication Data

Names: Deignan, Kathleen, 1947- editor. | Osgood, Libby, editor.
Title: Teilhard de Chardin : a book of hours / edited by Kathleen Deignan and Libby Osgood.
Other titles: Teilhard de Chardin (Maryknoll, N.Y.)
Description: Maryknoll, New York : Orbis Books, [2023] | Includes bibliographical references. | Summary: "Teilhard's words divided into a "Book of Hours" of eight days, according to Dawn, Day, Dusk, and Dark"—Provided by publisher.
Identifiers: LCCN 2022042461 (print) | LCCN 2022042462 (ebook) | ISBN 9781626985094 (print) | ISBN 9781608339716 (ebook)
Subjects: LCSH: Philosophy.
Classification: LCC B2430.T371 D38 2023 (print) | LCC B2430.T371 (ebook) | DDC 100—dc23/eng/20221026
LC record available at https://lccn.loc.gov/2022042461
LC ebook record available at https://lccn.loc.gov/2022042462

Throughout my life, by means of my life,
the world has little by little caught fire in my sight until,
aflame all around me,
it has become almost luminous from within.
Such has been my experience in contact with the Earth.
The diaphany of the Divine at the heart of the universe on fire.

Teilhard de Chardin (DM, 46)

For Elizabeth Scully, CND and Ann Moore, CND
and the many other teachers who brought us to Teilhard,
most especially Father Thomas Berry
who translated his cosmic vision into
The Great Work for our Living Earth and
Father John Battista Giuliani
whose sacramental ministry taught us to see.

—KD and LO, Feast of Pentecost, June 5, 2022

Contents

Saturday
Transforming Spirit

Tomorrow
Toward Omega

Foreword

Teilhard's Spiritual Vision

Mary Evelyn Tucker

This Book of Hours provides a fresh appreciation for Teilhard's comprehensive spiritual vision that is so deeply needed in our time. We are indebted to Kathleen Deignan and Libby Osgood for their painstaking work in opening up Teilhard's writing for daily contemplation.

SPIRIT AND MATTER

One of Teilhard's greatest contributions to modern religious thought is his conception of reality as composed of both spirit and matter. This is what he calls the psychic and the physical components of all reality, the within and the without of things.

Demonstrating that an interior and numinous dimension of matter is present from the beginning is Teilhard's aim. This radically alters our perspective of matter itself, which for him is not dead and inert but dynamic and evolving. In this context, the divine is no longer to be sought only in a transcendent union with a merciful God. Rather, there is a shift in our religious quest, which has previously been focused on otherworldly goals such as personal salvation after death.

Teilhard redirects our vision to what is close at hand and yet coextensive with the birth of the universe itself. The numinous reality that infuses matter brings us face-to-face with the immanence of the divine in all things. He observes that this essential spiritual dimension of the universe is the basis of a cosmic spirituality. He notes repeatedly that unless there were an interior aspect to matter, consciousness could not emerge in the human. The human, then, should not be seen as something extrinsic or added on to the evolutionary process, but as an emergent expression of what went before. To understand that all reality from the tiniest atom to the entire Earth community is composed of a within and a without gives us a very different perspective on our universe and our spiritual journey.

COSMIC PERSPECTIVE

The implications of this insight for spirituality can help to achieve a reciprocity with both the particular and the whole of the universe and the natural world in a way scarcely imagined until now. Traditionally, as noted, Christian hope rested in a transcendent union with the divine outside of the Earth or cosmos. Now that is balanced by a new understanding of immanence in the depths of matter. The interiority of matter finds its expression in the dynamic emergence of the cosmos over immense expanses of evolutionary time: from radiant plasma to the emergence of galaxies, from the dust clouds of supernovas to solar systems such as ours with the Earth, and from single cells to multicellular life, including humans.

Teilhard believed this dynamic evolutionary perspective would permit humans to appreciate anew the fundamental unity of life. He felt that knowledge of such a feeling for unity in the universe is dawning on human consciousness through the discoveries of science. A sense of the cosmos and Earth is again becoming a part of our collective imagination, as it was for indigenous peoples. Teilhard writes,

> The cosmic sense must have been born as soon as man found himself facing the forest, the sea and the stars. And since then we find evidence of it in all our experience of the great and unbounded: in art, in poetry, in religion. Through it we react to the world as a whole as with our eyes to the light.[1]

In terms of cosmic perspective, then, Teilhard offers a vision of unity that resituates the human in the whole evolutionary journey. It provides a means of reciprocity and reverence with

[1] *Human Energy*, trans. J. M. Cohen (New York: Harcourt Brace Jovanovich, 1971), 82.

the universe and Earth, which our contemporary scientific view of matter does not generally include. Matter or nature in modern reductive science is considered to be mechanistic and separate from the human. Our capacity for communication with nature is greatly enlarged and revitalized when we recognize its essential connectedness with ourselves. Surely this has important implications for our understandings of our larger purpose and sense of belonging.

THE CHALLENGE OF HUMAN PURPOSE

Purpose may be one of the greatest problems facing the contemporary human community. We have already witnessed considerable inroads into the purpose, or teleological thrust, of religion by existentialists and postmodern critics who wish to bracket out all concepts of shared purpose or values within evolutionary processes. Such critics speak of purposelessness in the universe mirrored by the apparent lack of direction so deeply embedded in individuals and in our society at large.

One may well ask what effect this has on contemporary spirituality. The answer is: a very significant one. If spirit and matter are the dynamics of evolution, we have a radically new perspective for situating the whole idea of purpose. No longer can the emergence of humans be viewed as simply a random event in an empty, purposeless universe. Rather we are intrinsically linked to the evolution of spirit and matter in the universe as a whole. In fact, we are at a moment in history when we are taking responsibility for guiding this evolutionary process in a sympathetic awareness of its profound connection to ourselves.

This especially challenges us to expand our idea of spirituality. As Teilhard advises, we need to embody this explicit consciousness of being an atom or a citizen of the universe. This sense of perspective and purpose is now so widely drawn in an evolutionary context as to be a dramatic challenge to all traditional spiritualities.

We are confronted with the task of resituating the world's religions, which embrace some five thousand years of history, into a perspective that reveals the universe to be fourteen billion years old. The imperative is to shift from human historical horizons to developmental cosmic and geological time. The epochal change is from the divine as simply transcendent to the world to a sense of the divine present and acting in the world. In this transition we move from seeing spirit and matter as always separate, to seeing human lives and destinies intertwined in evolution. We shift from a perspective that views the Logos as given from without, to one that begins to discover an inner ordering principle (Logos) at the heart of all matter. Indeed, this is how John's Gospel opens: "In the beginning was the Word [Logos]."

Our spiritual goals are thus reoriented from a quest toward otherworldly perfection and goodness to a quest toward aligning with the dynamic evolutionary processes close at hand. Our spiritual purpose is expanded to embrace and to understand both four and a half billion years of Earth history and the contemporary environmental challenges to the planet and the evolution of its life forms.

SPIRITUAL PRACTICE

If our sense of spiritual perspective and purpose has been expanded by Teilhard, what are the consequences for human action and spiritual practice? Teilhard's vision is eminently practical, not simply a misplaced abstraction for personal spiritual growth. Rather, his cosmological vision has consequences for spiritual practice in at least three ways: for prayer, sacrifice, and action.

With regard to prayer, Teilhard provides numerous examples of his mystical devotionalism, as this Book of Hours illustrates. Teilhard's cosmic perspective gives us a context in which to pray with and through all the elements in the universe. We can pray with a new organic and ecological sense of reverence. The winds, the stars, the waves, and fire become a symphony of praise to the divine—something the Psalmists, the writer of the Song of Solomon, St. Francis of Assisi, and Hildegard of Bingen understood intimately. This cosmic dimension of life in Christocentric prayer found early expression in the epistles of Paul, such as Ephesians, Colossians, and 1 Corinthians. In early modern Christianity, this cosmological sense of Christ waned and an emphasis on redemption predominated. This became widespread with the devotional *Imitation of Christ* treatise by Thomas à Kempis. We may now reintegrate a focus on the historical Christ of mercy with the Cosmic Christ, the Logos at the heart of the universe.

A sympathetic resonance with nature and an understanding of the Cosmic Christ become rich resources for prayer, worship, and meditation. To pray with all the elements and with matter itself becomes a way of drawing strength from the transformative powers of the evolutionary process. Finally, to pray in this enlarged context becomes a means of overcoming the powerful forces of alienation and impersonalism that pervade modern culture. We are indeed citizens of the universe and Earth, and our prayer may align with the dynamic changing powers of life in this extraordinary milieu. Teilhard gives us many examples of such an expanded mode of prayer, one of the most striking of which is his *Hymn of the Universe*. Here he offers his "Mass on the World" without bread or wine while on a scientific expedition in the Ordos Desert of China. Teilhard also wrote his powerful "Hymn to Matter," the divine milieu, which illustrates a new ecological mode of prayer: "I acclaim you as the divine milieu, charged with creative power, as the ocean stirred by the Spirit, as the clay molded and infused with life by the incarnate Word" (HU, 67).

In terms of sacrifice, Teilhard provides us with a frame that enlarges our understanding of traditional ideas. From the supreme sacrifice of Christ on the cross, Teilhard points to the sacrificial nature of the whole evolutionary process in which the human has a special role. Such a spirituality offers us the largest context possible to situate our own yearnings toward meaning. In this way, for Teilhard, sacrifice takes on a powerful cosmic dimension:

> Human suffering, the sum total of suffering poured out at each moment over the whole earth, is like an immeasurable ocean. But what makes up this immensity? Is it blackness, emptiness, barren wastes? No indeed; it is potential energy. Suffering holds hidden within it, in extreme intensity, the ascensional force of the world. The whole point is to set this force free by making it conscious of what it is capable.[2]

---

[2]*Hymn of the Universe*, trans. Gerald Vann (New York: Harper & Row, 1965), 93–94.

Finally, in terms of human action, Teilhard's spiritual vision has practical implications for dynamizing human energies. Drawing on the thought of Maurice Blondel, Teilhard affirms action in all reality as manifesting the unity of the evolving cosmos. Teilhard's concern is to activate a zest for life and a will to participate in evolution. These are major recurring themes in his writings. He felt that creative human action assists the evolutionary advance and applies to every field of enterprise—education, science, law, business, agriculture, and art—all of which are involved in a transforming process greater than themselves. How to activate human energy and consciousness to this connection was one of Teilhard's concerns for an efficacious spirituality.

PERSONALIZATION

Amid all of this, Teilhard was concerned that his spiritual vision might be misunderstood as an impersonal pantheistic union with the cosmos. He also recognized the growing tendency of the modern world to depersonalize reality. He observed that we cannot simply anthropomorphize the cosmos, nor can we easily embrace an impersonal cosmos. He realized that we are left straddling a heritage of personal deity, while groping toward a larger intuition of a numinous presence in the cosmos.

In earlier periods and in many world religions the universe was seen as a Cosmic Person. To reassert meaning for the human venture, Teilhard suggests that we must rediscover the personal in the cosmos. For him this is the Cosmic Christ of the universe, the Logos that is present from the beginning of time, as John's Gospel observes. He sees this as an act of reawakening both our primordial sense of the cosmos along with our ecological insight into nature. This points toward a new vision of the numinous dimension of matter itself, what he describes as the "divine milieu":

> Let us establish ourselves in the divine milieu. There we shall find ourselves where the soul is most deep and where the matter is most dense. There we shall discover, with the confluence of all its beauties, the ultra-vital, the ultra-sensitive, the ultra-active point of the universe. And, at the same time, we shall feel the plenitude of our powers of action and adoration effortlessly ordered within our deepest selves.[3]

One aspect of the centering power of nature to draw all elements together is known in the physical order as gravity. For Teilhard its counterpart in the human is love. Both of these become expressions for the attractive forces of centering, individualization, and personalization. Again Teilhard speaks eloquently in this regard: "Love is the most universal, the most tremendous and the most mysterious of the cosmic forces."[4]

---

[3] *The Divine Milieu: An Essay on the Interior Life*, trans. Bernard Wall (New York: HarperCollins, 1960), 93.
[4] *Human Energy*, 32.

His spiritual vision is one that brings us an expanded sense of cosmic perspective and a new sense of life purpose. Its effect, however, is eminently practical and personalized for it implies nothing less than spiritual practices for the dynamizing of human energies with a new spiritual hope.

In our modern period we are passing through a great change in the activation of human energies at the same time that we are experiencing a crisis of physical energy sources. With this in mind, Teilhard reflects on the possibilities of the new vision of the planetization of life that he offers for a comprehensive spirituality for our times:

> Indeed . . . the hope of the planetization of life is very much more than a mere matter of biological speculation. It is more of a necessity for our age than the discovery, which we so ardently pursue, of new sources of [physical] energy. It is this idea which can and must bring us the spiritual fire without which all material fires, so laboriously lighted, will presently die down on the surface of the thinking Earth: the fire inspiriting us with the joy of action and the zest for life.[5]

Here is Teilhard's spiritual testimony, one that inspires us with its optimism, draws us forward with its cosmic perspec-

---

[5] *The Future of Man*, trans. Norman Denny (New York: HarperCollins, 1964), 118.

tive, and provides a powerful sense of purpose. His vision is a source of hope and energy amid the formidable challenges facing us at present. As the twenty-first century unfolds, we are seeking such grounding so as to renew the face of the Earth.

Acknowledgments

Thanks are due to many who have supported the realization of our Teilhardian *Book of Hours*. We are grateful to Mary Evelyn Tucker, cofounder of the Yale Forum on Religion and Ecology, who invited its creation many years ago and offered an illuminating Foreword, and to our editor at Orbis Books, Jon Sweeney, who graciously brought it to publication. To our generous colleagues at Iona College, Research Librarian and masterful permissions assistant Sydni Meyer, and Rick Palladino, Director of Libraries: your service has been invaluable. A warm note of thanks to our colleagues and friends in the American Teilhard Association for their enthusiasm for our project, especially President Kathleen Duffy, SSJ. Thanks are due as well to all our sisters, friends, and communities who supported us in many ways as we brought this passion project to completion. It gives us joy to have Father John Giuliani's inspired sketches and image of Teilhard grace this *Book of Hours* whose own life and ministry drew so many into the *divine milieu*. Of course, we want to thank each other—Kathleen and Libby—for the blessing of our collaboration in the creation of this breviary "for those who love the world" (DM, 11).[1] And with profound gratitude to Père Teilhard for making it all necessary.

---

[1] The editors have used a system for referencing every quotation from Teilhard. See the back of the book for these "Abbreviations" and "References."

Introduction

A Book of Hours
for Those Who Love the World

Kathleen Deignan

What you hold in your hands is a devotional companion for postmodern contemplatives created from the inspired cosmo-poetics of one of the great visionaries of our planet, the Jesuit priest-scientist Pierre Teilhard de Chardin (1881–1955). At once an exacting geologist and an inspired religious visionary, Teilhard's life and ministry were dedicated to "those who love the world" (DM, 11), to whom he offered a way to bridge the difficult divide between the still emergent science of evolution and Christian faith. Born in the ecologically rich and formative Auvergne region of France, Teilhard's early scientific interests were fostered by his naturalist father, while his profound faith and spirituality were nurtured by his devout Catholic mother, whose inspiration led him to enter the Society of Jesus at age eighteen to begin intensive theological and later scientific training.

Teilhard's studies were interrupted by World War I, during which he volunteered to be a stretcher bearer, an experience that would change and guide the course of his life. It was from the blood-soaked battlefields of the European Front that Teilhard began to draft seminal notes that would later develop into his most celebrated essays and books. It was from the battlefield also that his own visionary sense of humankind's role in God's evolutionary design for the cosmos took shape.

Resuming his science studies after the war, Teilhard earned a degree in geology and soon became an avid paleoanthropologist, researching human beginnings. A prolific contributor to his field, he participated in the discovery of the early hominid Peking Man, a subspecies of Homo erectus (LT, 160), and uncovered several new fossil species while in Egypt, one of which was later named for him: "Teilhardi" (LE, 207). But Teilhard soon came to sense that his quest to understand the meaning of the human enterprise was not to be discovered in the archaic past, but by turning his exploration toward the emerging future.

The early twentieth century was a revolutionary moment for scientific research and discovery as the new paradigm of evolution began to impact all aspects of human understanding and experience, especially religion. Heir to Darwinian evolutionism, Teilhard was also a contemporary of George Le Maître—the Belgian priest who first proposed the "primeval atom" theory of cosmic beginnings later described as the "big bang." Teilhard was born two years after and died a week before the legendary Einstein, and shared his moment with other eminent scientists probing the mysteries of the cosmos. Teilhard was particularly sensitive to how their work would affect not simply questions of human origins but more so their impact on questions of human destiny, the nature of the universe, and divinity itself. Drawn into these controversies as both a scientist and mystic, Teilhard fashioned the question to which he would direct his life: "Who will give evolution its God?"

Wrestling with this *koan*, Teilhard began to lecture and write toward new horizons of understanding to offer a way for people of faith to comprehend and integrate the new science into a sacred worldview. However, such publicity brought him into conflict with his traditionalist Jesuit and Vatican superiors who found his theological proposals beyond the boundaries of his science and religiously unsettling. In 1923, while teaching in Paris at the Institut Catholique and in response to requests from students, Teilhard wrote a short essay titled "Note on Some Possible Historical Representations of Original Sin," attempting to help reconcile the biblical presentation of human origins with the new Darwinian understandings of evolution by proposing a more contemporary and scientifically relevant reading of the creation narratives of Genesis (CE, 46). When his private note for a few students and friends was reported to his Jesuit superiors, Teilhard found himself under interdict and summarily exiled to a Jesuit-sponsored science museum in China to focus exclusively on paleontology. Ironically, it was during his Asian exile that Teilhard helped to find fossil evidence for the theory of evolution.

Banishment did not silence Teilhard, however, but gave greater urgency to his commitment to write for the sake of "those who love the world" (DM, 11). Regrettably, the fruit of his most intense labor, his books *Le Milieu Divin* and *Le Phénomène Humain*, were not published during his lifetime, despite multiple requests to his order and many revisions. Yet he found a way to remain obedient both to superiors and his personal mission by bequeathing his writings to his secretary Jeanne Mortier, who saw to it that they were published after his death. When they were, the Holy Office still issued an official warning on June 30, 1962, regarding the ambiguities and errors against doctrine in Teilhard's writings. Even so, from the first publication of his extraordinary trove his message began to be broadly accepted and embraced across the religious and secular worlds, as decades later countless books, institutes, scholarly associations, conferences, curricula, courses, and retreats were dedicated to unfolding his rich legacy. Even popes have saluted him as a Christian seer for our time, most notably Pope Francis, who cites him in paragraph #83 of his papal encyclical, *Laudato si'*.

Vivid and reflective reports of Teilhard's travels around the globe can be found in his letters and essays from South Africa to Mongolia, Egypt to Paris, the badlands of Arizona, and lastly from his final years in New York. Pere Teilhard died in Manhattan on Easter Sunday, April 10, 1955, at the age of seventh-three and is buried in the cemetery of Saint Andrew's on the Hudson, a former Jesuit novitiate, now the Culinary Institute of America in Hyde Park. In all, Teilhard leaves a unique legacy of inspired religious writings, no fewer than 196 spiritual essays and books about his experience of finding God through the Earth and the cosmos and offering a visionary framework for our deepest human self-understanding. It is from this stunning library of luminous texts that the book you are holding was composed.

Offered in the form of a Book of Hours, this Teilhardian breviary promises to ignite one's innate sense of the universe as the revelatory and evolving body of divinity. This is a work of love, joyfully created with my Congregation of Notre Dame sister, Libby Osgood. She, a young engineer, and I, an elder theologian, have spent two years intensively combing through and dialoguing about Teilhard's literary corpus to capture the illuminating power of "found" prayers, poems, and hymns shining throughout his written legacy. Here, in this resource for daily prayer, we present them in an elegantly unified format to awaken in those who pray with them what was so palpably alive in Teilhard: the cosmic sense of the sacred.

However, this is not a book *about* the renowned priest-scientist who brought his challenge and genius to the divide between an ever more expansive scientific picture of the universe and uncomprehending static religious worldviews. Nor is it an investigation into Teilhard's original and challenging cosmic system to be unraveled intellectually. Such work continues to be ably done by an exceptional community of theologians, scientists, religious historians, biographers, and artistic interpreters. Comprising a growing Teilhardian School of thought, these scholars have worked to present his radical recasting of traditional worldviews in the light of evolutionary science illuminated by religious faith. His and their work have been dispersed broadly to significantly influence culture, education, religion, the arts, and new formularies of contemporary thought. Rather, the offering being made here is not the remarkable system of Teilhard the cosmological scientist, but the spirituality of Teilhard the cosmic mystic.

If you are new to the gift of Teilhard, we invite you to explore the website of the American Teilhard Association at www.teilharddechardin.org—a vibrant network that holds and unfolds his living legacy, founded by two of his earliest disciples and distinguished teachers in their own right, Father Thomas Berry and Dr. Ewert Cousins. There you will find an introduction and comprehensive résumé of Teilhard's life and work by eminent Teilhardians Mary Evelyn Tucker and John Grim.

Though students and teachers within this virtual school, my colleague and I depart from earlier waves of scholarship that have adopted explanatory or exploratory approaches to his work. We have chosen to be expository, using a singular lens to recognize and present the most incandescent cosmo-poetic writings from Teilhard's rich literary corpus that invite contemplatives into a new mind and heart to participate in the divine work of cosmogenesis. In the simple curation of this cache of literary gems, a singular timbre of Teilhard's voice is heard sounding as priest of the cosmos, visionary of a new religious conception, personal mentor, and guide for a critical and protracted era of global spiritual emergence.

Because it was Teilhard's explicit desire to offer succeeding generations an expansive spiritual horizon and the energy to reach it in the practice of integral, multifaceted worship, we sought motifs that serve his missionary purpose: to intensify humanity's capacity for adoration. Months of gleaning through his written collection were rewarded with a harvest of full-bodied language with which to understand, speak of, and most importantly to worship "evolution's God."

> I want these pages to be instinct with my love of matter and life and to reconcile it if possible with the unique adoration of and only absolute and definitive godhead. (WTW, 14)

So, as we labored to distill, harmonize, and augment Teilhard's stunning idiom of prayer, this unique breviary was born in a new voice of praise. It opens the contemplative to a sacred space for encountering Teilhard the Spiritual Master and companion for citizens of the universe who desire to awaken into the *divine milieu.*

"For those who love the world" comes from the dedication page of Teilhard's own singular spiritual masterpiece, *The Divine Milieu,* published in 1927. Written for the wayfarers of his time lost upon the shifting tides of a tumultuous century, Teilhard wished to offer his contemporaries and those to follow trustworthy orientation through the inevitable human challenges that marked the crisis of modernity and now its aftermath. On the whole, religions were failing to speak to the people of a dramatically new age entrenched in static worldviews and ideologies, political polarizations, planetary warfare, and world-shaking scientific discovery. In the absence of a common language of meaning, bifurcation continued to widen the divide between persons of religious instinct and a new breed of atheists who found faith within the world alone. But for Teilhard there was no such divergence. He believed we had come at last to a moment when humankind together might witness and realize greater convergence in all dimensions of human existence under the suasion of a new scientific/religious cosmology, a unitive insight that celebrated a way to love the world in God and God in the world.

But Teilhard's spiritual classic neither fulfilled nor exhausted his ministry to guide the "wayfarers" of the world toward their true nature as planetary citizens. Instead, it served as a kind of preamble to his mystical teachings redolent throughout the broad and complex literary corpus found among his books, essays, and particularly in his rich personal correspondence. In that spirit, this *Book of Hours* means to serve Teilhard's perennial desire to be spiritual mentor and guide to those who love the world by inviting us to pray and worship with him in a "cosmogonic" key as a way to activate a capacity to perceive and abide in the *divine milieu* as our true home ground.

The design of this breviary offers today's contemplatives a fresh way to pray, in Teilhard's own words, a centuries-old devotional practice organic in nature and one that finds its likeness in nearly every religious tradition. Honoring Earth's axial rotation and terrestrial rhythms, global cultures have designed patterns for consecrating time, for awakening spiritual senses, for entering into a thin space, a harbor of grace to keep us in peace and presence. In the Christian form such regular prayer patterns have a long and varied pedigree originally rooted in Judaic practice and flowering in the many patterns for Christian communal or solitary daily prayer. Sometimes called "The Liturgy of the Hours" or "The Divine Office," these devotional sequences serve to entrain a person to the spiritual opportunities offered in the shifting moods of an Earth day at once concealing and revealing the palpable presence of divinity in those intervals when our galactic mother star shines then veils her face: *dawn* turning to *day,* turning to *dusk,* turning to *dark.* As hours beget days, so this breviary ushers us into a week of deep reflection on the sacred mysteries illuminated by Teilhard's insight.

To give depth to this format of prayer we have invoked the creative tropes of "hexameron literature" popular in the medieval Christian period, a genre that presented theological and cosmological commentaries on the six days of biblical creation accounts interpreted in richly mystical and moral terms. Though largely faded from use, this literary formula affords a way to let Teilhard's creation days unfold—with one alteration. Instead of a six-day or seven-day imaginary, we offer an octameral formula of eight days: *Unfolding Cosmos, Evolving Christ, Living Earth, Becoming Human, Building the World, Creative Suffering, Transforming Spirit,* and an eighth day anticipating the cosmic climax *Toward Omega.*

This innovation imitates in a metaphorical way Teilhard's vision of ongoing creation in its full expanse from the genesis of the universe in its primordial first day, incrementally moving through deep time toward its future frontier, as yet unknown and unimaginable. In this all-embracing style the fullness of a divinely generative cosmos progressively unfurls through the week, day by day, hour by hour, to magnetize and mesmerize us, and activate our own desire to participate in the journey.

There's no doubt that there is a powerful educative force lodged in the world, which continually calls us to journey further into the deep layers of being: what attracts us in things is always withdrawing further from us, beyond every individual tangible reality, and finally beyond death. (MM, 296)

This life-changing journey motif is another archetypal trope that finds resonance in Teilhardian thought as a medium for the transformation of human nature. An eight-day spiritual itinerary for humans navigating the mysterious pathways of evolution harkens back to a variety of similar formulas in the Christian tradition. In the thirteenth century the Franciscan Master Bonaventure offered a guiding map for Christians wayfaring toward divinity in *The Mind's Journey into God*. Orientation patterns such as these work alongside other proposals for spiritual maturing exemplified most lastingly in the *Spiritual Exercises* of St. Ignatius of Loyola, developed to inform a disciple's process of realizing spiritual maturity and liberty. In this lineage, Teilhard offers guidance for fostering mystical ambition, though less systematically. Similarly, he proposes ascetical exercises to activate human transformation, though more suggestively.

Yet when we tune in to his "found" hymns of adoration and praise, his "found" epistles and exhortations, canticles and blessings, and when they become the focus of our *lectio divina*, we hear the voice of a master of souls who desires Christic transformation—the voice of a pastor, psalmist, mentor, and sage. Teilhard's voice is here for those who seek an inspired teacher with whom to learn to see as he did and as we may.

Seeing. One could say that the whole of life lies in seeing—
if not ultimately, at least essentially. To be more is to be
more united—and this sums up and is the very conclusion
of the work to follow. But unity grows . . . only if it is
supported by an increase of consciousness, of vision. That is
probably why the history of the living world can be reduced
to the elaboration of ever more perfect eyes at the heart of
a cosmos where it is always possible to discern more. Are
not the perfection of an animal and the supremacy of the
thinking being measured by the penetration and power
of synthesis of their glance? To try to see more and to
see better is not, therefore, just a fantasy, curiosity, or a
luxury. See or perish. This is the situation imposed on every
element of the universe by the mysterious gift of existence.
And thus, to a higher degree, this is the human condition.
(HP, 31)

Simultaneous with Teilhard's existential insight came an
understanding that he himself was someone with penetrating
eyes able to sense beneath the incoherence and confusions of
surface existence, a deep, living unity. With this self-recognition
he accepted a mandate that became his sacred mission: to generate a chain reaction of similar insight to spread explosively
around the world.

I do believe that I can see something, and I would like that
something to be seen. You can't imagine what intensity
of desire I sometimes feel in this connection, and what
impotence! (MM, 269)

And so he prays to be "the apostle, the evangelist" of his scientifically religious intuition concerning the multidimensionality of the living cosmos.

In particular, he desired to be the apostle of a life-transforming gospel announcing a vision of divinity laboring to self-manifest as the incarnate body of the world, perceived through his Christian eyes as the living Christ-force at play in the universe. The paleontologist turned from his professional quest to scientifically understand the human phenomenon by exploring its fossil past to something far more profound: his sense that the human species is an evolutionary force who brings into the universe something completely new. Feeling the inner pressure of such a cosmic "gospel" arising in him, he prayed to know how to awaken it in others. He perceived that this radical sense of human significance could be a catalyst for understanding the entire cosmic enterprise, even a new understanding of divinity. It would be "the dawn of a new epiphany" (TF, 38).

Teilhard could see from his deep-time perspective on an ever ancient–ever new cosmos that the human journey and our work on its behalf may be just beginning in earnest. To aid us on our tentative itinerary toward unitive convergence, he persuades us to accept our vocation to be the orienteers and "the arrow" of such consciousness evolution. He understood that a cosmic expedition required divestment of all distorting identities and prejudices of which he was aware—political, national, tribal, and religious. Only thus could he be liberated from ideological conditioning and psychological obscuration so that his true terrestrial identity could be sensed and lived. How often Teilhard repeated his creed, the simple utterance of a pure heart! "I am less a child of heaven than I am a child of earth" (HU, 13).

In service of "earth's task" Teilhard asks for an augmentation of the traditional Christian gospels that strive to engender personal, interpersonal, and social morality. Teilhard's new testament calls for conversions toward ecological morality and mysticism arising from a more penetrating sense of the continuing incarnational process. For Teilhard to "work at earth's task" means asking disruptive questions, moving beyond obstructive answers, and generating creative alternatives.

He also indicates the course correction that could reorient us through the impasse to which our momentous wrong turn into materialist/technological captivity has brought us. Returning to the wisdom of cosmic realism he exhorts us to comprehend and generate the only actual energy that will power our long journey through the universe.

> This is the very moment, paradoxically, for Man to discover the biological value . . . of the only energy which can group and achieve . . . Man, without turning him into a gadget or a slave: a mutual form of love, based on the consciousness of a common Something (or rather Somebody) into which all together we converge. (LTF, 145)

With this we come to the heart of Teilhard's gospel and its upending of all spiritual dualisms, its healing of mystical double vision: "the essence of my 'gospel' can be summarized by these simple words: not only 'God is love' but 'the World is love' "

(LLS, 218). In its reception we are empowered to experience these mysteries as one and the same modalities of communion. Such unitive intimacy awakens the "cosmic sense" as love moves toward more vast horizons, beyond the human or even the terrestrial, reaching to the dynamic cosmos. With Teilhard we learn to love the universe in its totality, "its energies, its secrets, and its hopes because I am dedicated to God the only origin, the only issue, the only term" (WTW, 14).

Teilhard wished to activate in planetary amateurs the soul of a magnanimous lover fully alive with resonant attraction to all that is beautiful, mysterious, and suffering in the world. His understanding of loving goes beyond romantic, familial, or tribal bonding, because love neither originates nor culminates in the human. It is a cosmic power, a centrating magnetism like gravity itself that makes the ever expanding universe cohere. Love is a constructive, creative, unitive force born of the cosmos' own genius drawing all elements into convergence by all that is most intimate and ultimate in them. In the human, the conscious activation and guidance of this process becomes our species' highest vocation, our most arduous task, our evolutionary destiny.

Teilhard tells his spiritual novices that we shall be astonished at what depths of affection our conscious relationship to the universe will awake as we intentionally enter into the work and spirit of "amorization" (HM, 50). Guiding his disciples to understand more profoundly that it is divinity's own self that allures us in the face and form of the cosmos, he suggests that "there are infinite degrees in the loving initiation of one person into another unfathomable Person" (WTW, 147). To support such evolutionary transformation, the spiritual master invites our readiness to make a cosmic vow, indeed a Christic vow, in imitation of divine, self-emptying love: "the reckless vow of all love" through which we lose ourselves in all that we love ever more intimately and expansively (DM, 132).

"The reckless vow of all love" reveals to those who love the world another hidden power of the universe. In Teilhard's experience, nothing exhilarates human creatures more than the joy of finding and surrendering to a beauty greater than ourselves discovered in the cosmic *process* that reveals a cosmic *presence* seen as a divine *person*. As mystery reveals itself to us universally, we feel surrounded by it, become transfixed by it "so that there is no room left to fall down and adore it, even within ourselves" (DM, 112).

Finding the world in our souls is the ground of our hope in an evolutionary, unfinished, suffering universe still laboring for liberation from the limitations and determinisms of being such. Yet it means we are congenitally, courageously oriented toward an unimaginable future, an unimaginable God of the future, an unimaginable human transfiguration in the future. Teilhard says we need a new face of God to worship, to astonish, to allure, and to inspire our adoration forward as we continue our perilous journey. Perhaps now we begin "to see" such an image dawning as we gradually realize our own mystical capacities empowered by a great faith in the God of tomorrow and in ourselves as embryonic agents of the future (AE, 238). Indeed, the new face of emerging divinity may yet be perceived as humankind converges in the sacred sphere of adoration to intone together God's newly whispered names.

As we chant our deepest desires in songs at dawn and in nightly hymns, we ourselves become enchanted as we attune to galactic choirs silently or plainly sounding throughout the *divine milieu*. With them we play into harmonies as yet unheard, augmenting the hymn of the universe being sung through everything calling us to offer the soaring descant and contrabass of our human voice. This Book of Hours offers those who love the world Teilhard's libretto. May it be a grace for you and for our living Earth through which such healing praise shall quietly resound.

Lex orandi, lex vivendi: As we pray, so we live.

Sunday

Unfolding Cosmos

Dawn

The whole universe is aflame.

INVOCATION

See, the universe is ablaze!
See how the starry depths expand
in an ever-vaster magazine of assembled suns.

DOXOLOGY

You, and You alone
are the entire and proper object of our love.
You, and You alone
are the creative energy that fathoms the secrets of our hearts
and the mystery of our growth.
By You, and You alone, our souls are awakened.

Opening Verse

This unique privilege of the cosmic sense expressed in love
is a bottomless ocean into which we can plunge indefinitely.

Hymn

Crimson gleams of Matter,
gliding imperceptibly into the gold of Spirit,
ultimately become transformed into the within
of every being and every event.
A progressive expansion of a mysterious inner clarity
transfigured them.

But, what was more,
there was a gradual variation of intensity and color
that was related to the complex interplay
of three universal components:

the Cosmic, the Human, and the Christic.

These asserted themselves explicitly in me
from the very first moments of my existence,
but it has taken me years of ardent effort
to discover that they were no more
than the successive heraldings or incandescence
of a Universe that is Person.

And through all this there blows,
animating it and spreading over it,
a fragrant balm,
a zephyr of Union and of the Feminine:

the Diaphany of the Divine
at the heart of a glowing Universe.

I have experienced it through contact with the Earth—
the Divine radiating from the depths of a blazing Matter.

ANTIPHON

God is the atmosphere in which we are bathed.

PSALM

God whom we try to apprehend by the groping of our lives
is as pervasive and perceptible as the atmosphere
in which we are bathed.
God encompasses us on all sides, like the world itself.

What prevents you, then, from enfolding God in your arms?
Only one thing: your inability to see God.

Without mixture, without confusion,
the true God will, under your gaze,
invade the universe.

God will penetrate it as a ray of light does a crystal;
and with the help of the great layers of creation,
will become for you universally perceptible and active,
very near and very distant at one and the same time.

Antiphon

In God and God alone the reckless vow of all love is realized.

Psalm

The delight of the *divine milieu*
(heavy with responsibilities)
is that it can assume an ever-increasing intensity around us.

One could say that it is an atmosphere
ever more luminous and ever more charged with God.

It is in God and in God alone
that the reckless vow of all love is realized:
to lose oneself in what one loves,
to sink oneself in it more and more.

If we want the *divine milieu* to grow all around us,
then we must jealously guard and nourish all the forces
of union, of desire, and of prayer that grace offers us.

By the mere fact that our transparency will increase,
the divine light, that never ceases to press in upon us,
will erupt the more powerfully.

Psalm Prayer

By means of all created things, without exception,
the divine assails us, penetrates us and molds us.
We imagined it as distant and inaccessible,
whereas in fact we live steeped in its burning layers.

Reading

A cosmic movement (or cosmogenesis); which takes the more
exact form of an organic movement (or biogenesis); and is itself completed in a reflective movement (or anthropogenesis).
Three movements, or more accurately three phases of one and
the same movement. It has become impossible to present the
world to us in the form of an established harmony: we now see
unmistakably that it is a system in movement. It is no longer an
order but a process. No longer a cosmos but a cosmogenesis. In
obedience to the laws of gravity a powdery matter first twists
itself into galaxies and ultimately coalesces into distinct stars,
within space. The main axis of the world in movement: why
should it not be a line running from atoms to stars?

Versicle

Far from light emerging gradually
out of the womb of our darkness,
it is the Light, existing before all else was made
which, patiently, surely, eliminates our darkness.

Responsory

The human soul,
deeply moved by the harmony of this divine world,
is vibrant with a mystical ambition.

Cosmic Canticle

Glorious Lord Christ:

Divine influence
secretly diffused and active in the depths of matter,
and the dazzling center
where all the innumerable fibers of the manifold meet—
power as implacable as the world and as warm as life.

You whose forehead is of the whiteness of snow,
whose eyes are of fire,
and whose feet are brighter than molten gold;

You whose hands imprison the stars;
You who are the first and the last,
the living and the dead and the risen again;

You who gather into Your exuberant unity
every beauty, every affinity,
every energy, every mode of existence:

It is You to whom my being cried out
with a desire as vast as the universe—
"In truth You are my Lord and my God."

~Intercessions~

Lord's Prayer

Lord of my childhood and Lord of my last days,
God, complete in Yourself
yet, for us, continually being born,
God, You offer Yourself to our worship as *evolver and evolving*,
the only being that can satisfy us.

Sweep away at last the clouds that still hide You,
the clouds of hostile prejudice and of false creeds.

You have become for my mind and heart
much more than God who was and who is:
You have become God who shall be.

Closing Prayer

Take possession of me, my God,
You who are more remote than all and deeper than all.
Take to Yourself and unite together
the immensity of the world
and the intimate depths of myself.

Day

*On the cosmic scale, only the fantastic
has a chance of being true.*

INVOCATION

See, the universe is ablaze!
How life draws from ever more distant sources
the sap that flows through its innumerable branches.

DOXOLOGY

You, and You alone
are the entire and proper object of our love.
You, and You alone
are the creative energy that fathoms the secrets of our hearts
and the mystery of our growth.
By You, and You alone, our souls are awakened.

Exhortation

Either the world is no more than appearance
or else it is in itself a part, an aspect, or a phase of God.
Respect the mystical requirements
of a supremely "communicating" universe.

Antiphon

See the divine welling up and showing through.

Psalm

All around us,
to right and left, in front and behind, above and below,
we have only had to go a little beyond the frontier
of sensible appearances
in order to see the divine welling up and showing through.

But it is not only close to us, in front of us,
that the divine presence has revealed itself.

It has sprung up so universally,
and we find ourselves so surrounded and transfixed by it,
that there is no room left to fall down and adore it,
even within ourselves.

Psalm Prayer

In the cosmos, as described here,
it becomes possible, strange though the expression appears,
to love the universe.
It is indeed in this act alone
that love can develop in boundless light and power.

Meditation

In the life which wells up in me
and in the matter which sustains me,
I find much more than Your gifts.

It is You Yourself whom I find,
You who makes me participate in Your being,
You who molds me.

Truly in the ruling and in the first disciplining
of my living strength,
in the continually beneficent play of secondary causes,
I touch, as near as possible,
the two faces of Your creative action,
and I encounter and kiss Your two marvelous hands—

the one which holds us so firmly
that it is merged, in us, with the sources of life,
and the other whose embrace is so wide

that, at its slightest pressure,
all the springs of the universe respond harmoniously together.

<u>PRAYER</u>

My God, all joy and all achievement,
the very purpose of my being
and all my love of life,
all depend on this one basic vision
of the union between Yourself and the universe.

~<u>REFLECTION</u>~

<u>LESSON</u>

Like particles immersed in one and the same spiritual
fluid, souls cannot think or pray or act or move, without waves
being produced, even by the most insignificant among them,
which set the others in motion; inevitably, behind each soul a
wake is formed which draws other souls either towards good
or towards evil.

<u>COLLECT</u>

The Universe stimulates the "*zest for being,*"
and provides the nourishment
which are transformed into love of God.
This process is extremely clear:
Heaven cannot dispense with Earth.

13

Examen

The pure heart is the heart that not only loves God above all things but sees God present throughout all things.

Kyrie

There is not matter and spirit.

All that exists is matter becoming spirit. *Kyrie Eleison*
There is neither spirit nor matter in the world.

The "stuff of the universe" is spirit-matter. *Christe Eleison*
No other substance but this

could produce the human molecule. *Kyrie Eleison*

Benediction

May Life become for you
not just some blind, favorable fatality,
but a kind of living Presence or Benevolence
in which it will be possible for you not only to trust
but to confide.

Come to be imbued with the conviction that the Universe
in us and around us is ultimately a great birth,
at the heart of a gradual quickening
which nothing can escape.
Explore this path
and the fundamental, unassailable joy to which it leads.

Dusk

What is emerging in us is the great cosmos.

INVOCATION

See, the universe is ablaze!
How there is an endless increase in our perception
of the hidden forces that lie dormant,
of the seething multitudes of the infinitesimal,
of the things that are so vast.

DOXOLOGY

You, and You alone
are the entire and proper object of our love.
You, and You alone
are the creative energy that fathoms the secrets of our hearts
and the mystery of our growth.
By You, and You alone, our souls are awakened.

15

Opening Verse

Plunge boldly into the vast current of things
and see whither its flow is carrying us.

Evening Hymn

In the beginning was Power,
intelligent, loving, energizing.

In the beginning was the Word,
supremely capable of mastering and molding
whatever might come into being in the world of matter.

In the beginning there were not coldness and darkness:
there was the Fire. This is the truth.

Antiphon

Everything means both everything and nothing to me;
everything is God to me and everything is dust.

Psalm

At the center of the *divine milieu,*
all the sounds of created being are fused,
without being confused,
in a single note which dominates and sustains them
(that seraphic note, no doubt, which bewitched St. Francis).

So all the powers of the soul begin to resound
in response to its call;
and these multiple tones, in their turn, compose themselves
into a single, ineffably simple vibration
in which all the spiritual nuances—

of love and of the intellect,
of zeal and of tranquility,
of fullness and of ecstasy,
of passion and of indifference,
of assimilation and of surrender,
of rest and of motion—

are born and pass and shine forth,
according to the times and the circumstances,
like the countless possibilities of an inward attitude,
inexpressible and unique.

And if any words could translate
that permanent and lucid intoxication better than others,
perhaps they would be "passionate indifference."

Everything means both everything and nothing to me;
everything is God to me and everything is dust to me:

that is what we can say with equal truth,
in accord with how the divine ray falls.

ANTIPHON

The world is filled, and filled with the Absolute.

PSALM

There is but a single fundamental feeling
underlying all mystical systems;
and that is an innate love of the human person,
extended to the whole universe.

The Presence that spreads through all things
is the only source that gives me light
and the only air that I can ever breathe.

The world is filled, and filled with the Absolute.
To see this is to be made free.

PSALM PRAYER

Those who have once experienced this vision
can never forget it.
The flash that opened their eyes remains as a light
imprinted deep within them; and they never cease to thrill
to the awareness of contact with the universe.

EPISTLE

It may be that for certain people faith is accompanied by some
compelling belief, by evidence, by pure joy. I understand it

18

more as a kind of calm world view in which everything is il-luminated and becomes livable, indefinitely, increasingly.

This act requires both a passive sensitization of the mind in order to see and a positive act of the will in order to try to achieve the point of view. Practically, I think that every one who is true to their ideal arrives in a similar way at the same adoration of That which conducts and unifies the World.

~Silence~

Responsory

The immensity of God is the essential attribute
which allows us to seize God everywhere,
within us and around us.

Cosmic Canticle

Focus your soul's eyes
so as to perceive this magnificence,
the mounting significance of the earth.

Your one thought will be to exclaim:

Greater still, Lord,
let Your universe be greater still,
so that I may hold You
and be held by You
by a contact at once made ever more intense
and ever wider in its extent!

LORD'S PRAYER

Lord of my childhood and Lord of my last days,
God, complete in Yourself
yet, for us, continually being born,
God, You offer Yourself to our worship as *evolver and
    evolving,*
the only being that can satisfy us.

Sweep away at last the clouds that still hide You,
the clouds of hostile prejudice and of false creeds.

You have become for my mind and heart
much more than God who was and who is:
You have become God who shall be.

CLOSING PRAYER

God must be as vast as the Universe
and as warm as a human heart,
and incomparably more besides.
This is all we can say.

Dark

*Live in the explicit consciousness of being
an atom or a citizen of the universe.*

INVOCATION

See, the universe is ablaze!
In very truth, it is God, and God alone
whose Spirit stirs up the whole mass of the universe
in ferment.

DOXOLOGY

You, and You alone
are the entire and proper object of our love.
You, and You alone
are the creative energy that fathoms the secrets of our hearts
and the mystery of our growth.
By You, and You alone, our souls are awakened.

Opening Verse

Deeper than the soul of individuals,
vaster than the human group,
there is a vital fluid or spirit of things,
there is some absolute that draws us and yet lies hidden.

Night Hymn

It is in the blaze of a universal translucence
and a universal conflagration
that I shall know the bliss of closing my eyes.

Energy transforming itself into presence.

It would appear that a single ray of such a light,
falling upon the noosphere,
would inevitably produce an explosion
powerful enough instantaneously
to set ablaze and refashion the face of the earth.

Antiphon

How great is the mystery
in which we are forever incorporated!

Night Psalm

We live at the center of the network of cosmic influences
as we live at the heart of the human crowd

or among the myriads of stars,
without, alas, being aware of their immensity.

We shall be astonished at the extent and the intimacy
of our relationship with the universe.

Where are the roots of our being?
They plunge back and down into the unfathomable past.

How great is the mystery of the first cells
which were one day animated by the breath of our souls!

How impossible to decipher
the welding of successive influences
in which we are forever incorporated!

In each one of us, through matter,
the whole history of the world is in part reflected.

ANTIPHON

Our soul is penetrated by the flow of cosmic influences.

NIGHT PSALM

Our soul is indebted to an inheritance
worked upon from all sides before ever it came into being
by the totality of the energies of the earth.

It feels, in its turn, besieged and penetrated
by the flow of cosmic influences
which have to be ordered and assimilated.

Let us look around us:
the waves come from all sides
and from the farthest horizon.

Through every cleft
the world we perceive floods us with its riches—
food for the body, nourishment for the eyes,
harmony of sounds and fullness of the heart,
unknown phenomena and new truths.

All these treasures, all these stimuli, all these calls,
coming to us from the four corners of the world,
cross our consciousness at every moment.

Psalm Prayer

God, who is as immense and all-embracing as matter,
and at the same time as warm and intimate as a soul,
is the Center who spreads through all things.

~Silence~

Litany

You do more than simply stand apart from things
as their Master,

You are more than the incommunicable splendor
of the universe.

You are, too, the dominating influence
that penetrates us, holds us, and draws us,
through the inmost core
of our most imperative and most deep-rooted desires.

You are the cosmic Being who envelops us and fulfils us
in the perfection of Your Unity.

It is, in all truth, in this way, and for this
that I love You above all things.

CLOSING PRAYER

No words can express the bliss
of feeling oneself possessed, absorbed, without end or limit,
by an Infinite that is not rarefied and colorless,
but living and luminous,
an Infinite that knows and attracts and loves.

Monday

Evolving Christ

Dawn

The Flesh of Christ is fed by the whole universe.

INVOCATION

Christ! Reveal Yourself
in the depths of our hearts,
as the Shepherd, the Animator, of the Universe.

DOXOLOGY

Through You, all bodies come together,
exert influence upon one another
and sustain one another
in the unity of the all-embracing sphere,
the confines of whose surface outrun our imagination.

Opening Verse

I can preach only the mystery of Your flesh,
You the Soul shining forth through all that surrounds us.

Hymn

Disperse, O Jesus, the clouds with your lightning!
Show yourself to us
as the Mighty, the Radiant, the Risen!

Come to us once again as the Pantocrator
who filled the solitude of the cupolas in the ancient basilicas!

Nothing less than this Parousia is needed
to counter-balance and dominate in our hearts
the glory of the world that is coming into view.

And so that we should triumph over the world with you,
come to us clothed in the glory of the world.

Antiphon

Ardent life of Christ, source of all our good.

Psalm

In Christ there was not simply a human—
there was *the human*;

not only the perfect human, the ideal human—
but *the total human,*
the one who gathered together,
in the depth of his consciousness,
the consciousness of all.

In virtue of this,
Christ's experience had to extend to the universal.

Let us try to gather together in one single ocean
the whole mass of passions, of anticipations,
of fears, of sufferings, of happiness,
of which each of us represents one drop.

It was into this vast sea that Christ plunged,
so as to absorb it, through all his pores, in his entire person.

It was this storm-tossed sea
that Christ diverted into his mighty heart,
there to make its waves and tides
subject to the rhythm of his own life.

That is the meaning of the ardent life of Christ,
Christ the source of all our good,
of Christ as he prays;

and therein lies the unfathomable secret of his agony,
and the incomparable virtue, too,
of his death on the Cross.

Faith in the universal Christ is inexhaustibly fruitful.

PSALM

All around us, Christ is physically active in all things.

From the ultimate vibration of the atom
to the loftiest mystical contemplation;
from the lightest breeze that ruffles the air
to the broadest currents of life and thought,
he ceaselessly animates, without disturbing,
all the earth's processes.

And in return
Christ gains physically from every one of them.

Everything that is good in the universe
(everything that goes towards unification through effort)
is gathered up by the Incarnate Word
as a nourishment that it assimilates,
transforms and divinizes.

Faith in the universal Christ
is inexhaustibly fruitful
in the moral and mystical fields.

Psalm Prayer

There lies hidden beneath the ascending movement of life,
the continuous action of a being
who raises up the universe from within.

Reading

The whole problem now is to determine the truth and the
name of the presence that we believe we can feel behind the
blaze of the universe. If there is in truth at the other end of
cosmic duration Some Thing or Some One towards whom we
are advancing, then we must contrive to know its nature better,
so that we may the better worship.

Versicle

The universe takes on the lineaments of Jesus.
Christ is loved as a person;
Christ compels recognition as a world.

~Silence~

Responsory

The world manifests itself to the mystic
as bathed in an inward light
which brings out its structure, its relief, its depths.

Cosmic Canticle

Rich with the sap of the world,
I rise up towards the Spirit
whose vesture is the magnificence of the material universe
but who smiles at me from far beyond all victories.

And, lost in the mystery of the flesh of God,
I cannot tell which is the more radiant bliss:

to have found the Word
and so be able to achieve the mastery of matter,
or to have mastered matter
and so be able to attain and submit to the light of God.

~Intercessions~

Lord's Prayer

Lord of my childhood and Lord of my last days,
God, complete in Yourself
yet, for us, continually being born,
God, You offer Yourself to our worship as *evolver and evolving,*
the only being that can satisfy us.

Sweep away at last the clouds that still hide You,
the clouds of hostile prejudice and of false creeds.

You have become for my mind and heart
much more than God who was and who is:
You have become God who shall be.

Closing Prayer

Christ consumes with a glance my entire being.
And with that same glance, that same presence,
Christ enters into those who are around me and whom I love.
Christ binds us and reveals us to one another.

Day

Christ is loved as a person:
Christ compels recognition as a world.

Invocation

Lord, make of each of us a purifying leaven,
through the activity of the Child-God!

Doxology

Through You, all bodies come together,
exert influence upon one another
and sustain one another
in the unity of the all-embracing sphere,
the confines of whose surface outrun our imagination.

Exhortation

We can never know
all that the Incarnation still asks
of the world's potentialities.
We can never hope for too much
from the growing unity of humankind.

We must try everything for Christ;
we must hope everything for Christ.

Antiphon

Christ: the inner life and light of the world.

Psalm

Christ is the plenitude of the universe,
its principle of synthesis,
something more than all the elements
of this world put together.

And then comes the question—
who is Christ?

Christ is not something added to the world as an extra,
is not an embellishment.

Christ is the alpha and the omega,
the principle and the end,
the foundation stone and the keystone,
the Plenitude and the Plenifier.

Christ is the one who consummates all things
and gives them their consistence.
It is towards Christ and through Christ,
the inner life and light of the world,
that the universal convergence of all created spirit
is effected in sweat and tears.

Christ is the single center, precious and consistent,
who glitters at the summit that is to crown the world,
at the opposite pole from
those dim and eternally shrinking regions
into which our science ventures
when it descends the road of matter and the past.

PSALM PRAYER

The Christ who gradually self-reveals
is not a phantasy nor a symbol;
Christ is the reality of what,
through the whole structure of human activity,
we are awaiting.

Meditation

God did not will individually,
the sun, the earth, plants, or humanity.
God willed His Christ.

And in order to have Christ,
God had to create the spiritual world,
and humanity in particular,
upon which Christ might germinate.

And to have humanity,
God had to launch the vast process of organic life
which is an essential organ of the world.
And the birth of that organic life
called for the entire cosmic turbulence.

Prayer

Under our very eyes, and in our hearts,
Christ-the-Redeemer is being fulfilled and unfolding
in the figure of Christ-the-Evolver.

~Reflection~

Lesson

Under the constant flood of being that science lets loose, a certain small-scale academic Christ is swept away; and instead, the great Christ of tradition and mysticism is revealed and must be accepted. And it is to this Christ that we must turn. If Christ is to be truly universal, the Redemption, and hence the Fall, must extend to the whole universe.

COLLECT

To be the alpha and omega,
Christ must, without losing His precise humanity,
become co-extensive with the physical expanse
of time and space.
In order to reign on earth,
Christ must *super-animate* the world.

In Christ henceforth, by the whole logic of Christianity,
personality expands (or rather centers itself)
till it becomes universal.

Is this not exactly the God we are waiting for?

EXAMEN

We must try to penetrate our most secret self, and examine our being from all sides. Let us try, patiently, to perceive the ocean of forces to which we are subjected and in which our growth is steeped. This is a salutary exercise, for the depth and universality of our dependence on so much outside our control go to make up the embracing intimacy of our communion with the world to which we belong.

Kyrie

Christ manifesting, not hidden in clouds,
  but clothed in the energies of the world. *Kyrie Eleison*
Christ, no longer the condemner but the Savior
  of the modern world, its hopes in the future. *Christe Eleison*
Such a Christ would immediately draw to Himself the vital
  part of humankind. *Kyrie Eleison*

Benediction

May my acceptance be ever more complete,
more comprehensive, more intense.

May my being, in its self-offering to You,
become ever more open and more transparent
to Your influence.

May I thus feel Your activity coming ever closer,
Your presence growing ever more intense,
everywhere around me.

Fiat, fiat.

Dusk

*Christ is the physical center
of the gathering together of souls in God.*

INVOCATION

Let Your universal Presence spring forth
in a blaze that is at Once Diaphany and Fire.
O ever-greater Christ!

DOXOLOGY

Through You, all bodies come together,
exert influence upon one another
and sustain one another
in the unity of the all-embracing sphere,
the confines of whose surface outrun our imagination.

I have become a living particle of the Body of Christ,
all that affects me must help the growth of the total Christ.

Evening Hymn

With ever the same brilliance in all,
Christ shines as a light
at the heart of every life,
at the ideal term of every growth.

Everywhere Christ draws us and brings us closer,
in a universal movement of convergence towards Spirit.

It is Christ alone whom we seek
and in whom we move.

But if we are to hold Christ
we must take all things to and beyond the utmost limit
of their nature and their capacity for progress.

Of the cosmic Christ,
we may say both that Christ is
and is entering into fuller being.

Antiphon

Christ consecrated the integrity of Mother Earth.

Psalm

Nothing can enter into the universe
that does not emerge from it.
Nothing can be absorbed into things
except through the road of matter,
by ascent from plurality.

For Christ to enter into the world
by any side-road would be incomprehensible.

The Redeemer could penetrate the stuff of the cosmos,
could pour into the life-blood of the universe,
only by first dissolving in matter,
later to be reborn from it.

Christ did not lessen, but consecrated
the integrity of Mother Earth.

The smallness of Christ in the cradle,
and the even tinier forms
that preceded Christ's appearance among humanity,
are more than a moral lesson in humility.

They are in the first place
the application of a law of birth
and the sign of Christ definitively taking possession
of the world.

It is because Christ was *inoculated* in matter
that Christ can no longer be dissociated
from the growth of Spirit.

Christ is so engrained in the visible world
that Christ could henceforth be torn away from it
only by rocking the foundations of the universe.

ANTIPHON

The heart of the world is caught in the heart of God.

PSALM

When all the things around me,
preserving their own individual contours,
their own special savors,

appear to me as animated by a single secret spirit
diffused and intermingled within a single element,
infinitely close, infinitely remote,

and when, locked within the jealous intimacy
of a divine sanctuary,

I yet feel myself to be wandering at large
in the empyrean of all created beings.

Then I shall know that I am approaching that central point
where the heart of the world
is caught in the descending radiance
of the heart of God.

Psalm Prayer

Whatever we do, it is to Christ we do it.
Whatever is done to us, it is Christ who does it.
Like a powerful organism,
the world transforms me into the One who animates it.
Christ holds us by the most material fibers of nature.

Epistle

It gives me pleasure that you are rediscovering the Son in the
New Testament. However, I will say this: I do not like that
evangelism which limits itself to a glorification of the purely
human or moral qualities of Jesus. If Jesus were no more than a
father, a mother, a brother, a sister to us, I would not have need
of him; and, in a sense, the past does not interest me. What I
ask is that Christ be a Force that is immense, present, universal,
as real (more real) than Matter, which I can adore; in short, I
ask Christ to be for me the Universe: complete, concentrated,
and capable of being adored.

This is why, while acknowledging the irreplaceable value of
the first three Gospels in presenting the real, historical beginnings of Christ, I prefer Saint John and Saint Paul, who really

present in the resurrected Christ a being as vast as the World of all time.

Have you read the beginning of the Epistle to the Colossians (1:12–23), and tried to give it the full, organic meaning it requires? Here Christ appears as a true soul of the World. It is only thus that I love Christ.

~SILENCE~

RESPONSORY

I live at the heart of a single, unique Element,
the Center of the universe and present in each part of it:
personal Love and cosmic Power.

COSMIC CANTICLE

The earth's crust has not yet stopped heaving
and plunging under our feet.
Mountain ranges are still being thrust up on the horizon.
Granites are still growing under the continental masses.
Nor has the organic world ceased to produce new buds
at the tips of its countless branches.

Grace is the sap which, rising in the one trunk,
spreads through all the veins
in obedience to the pulsations of the one heart.

It is the nerve-impulse flowing through all the members
at the command of the one brain.

And the radiant Head, the mighty Heart, the fruitful Tree
are, of necessity, Christ.

~INTERCESSIONS~

LORD'S PRAYER

Lord of my childhood and Lord of my last days,
God, complete in Yourself
yet, for us, continually being born,
God, You offer Yourself to our worship as *evolver and evolving,*
the only being that can satisfy us.

Sweep away at last the clouds that still hide You,
the clouds of hostile prejudice and of false creeds.

You have become for my mind and heart
much more than God who was and who is:
You have become God who shall be.

CLOSING PRAYER

Christ has already appeared in the world;
but a long process of growth awaits Christ in this world,
either in isolated individuals or in human spiritual unity
of which our present society is no more than an adumbration.

The whole function, task, and drama of the universe,
the whole economy of human progress,
take on their ultimate significance
in this individualization of the Universal Element
in which the Incarnation consists.

Dark

I dream going to God under the pressure
of the strongest and the wildest spirits of the world.

INVOCATION

Christ, flood into and over me,
me and my cosmos.
How I long, Lord Christ, for this to be!

DOXOLOGY

Through You, all bodies come together,
exert influence upon one another
and sustain one another
in the unity of the all-embracing sphere,
the confines of whose surface outrun our imagination.

Opening Verse

Christ is clothed in the earth:
let this earth, then, grow ever greater,
that Christ's raiment may be ever more magnificent!

Night Hymn

The figure of Christ emerges:
it takes on definition in the midst of our nebula
of participated beings and secondary causes.

The universe assumes the form of Christ—
but, O mystery!
The one we see is Christ crucified.

Christ is the goad
that urges creatures along the road
of effort, of elevation, of development.

Christ is that mightier life
that inexorably brings death to our base egoisms
in order to draw into itself all our capacities for loving.

Antiphon

Everything around me has become for me
the substance of your heart: Jesus!

Night Psalm

Every presence makes me feel that you are near me;
every touch is the touch of your hand;
every necessity transmits to me a pulsation of your will.
Jesus!

And so true is this,
that everything around me
that is essential and enduring
has become for me
the dominance and the substance of your heart:
Jesus!

In the mystery of your mystical body
—your cosmic body—
you sought to feel the echo
of every joy and every fear
that moves each single one of all the countless cells
that make up humankind.
Jesus!

When I think of you, Lord, I cannot say
whether it is in this place that I find you more,
or in that place—
whether you are to me Friend or Strength or Matter—
whether I am contemplating you or whether I am suffering—
whether I rue my faults or find union—
whether it is you I love or the whole sum of others.

Every affection, every desire, every possession,
every light, every depth, every harmony, and every ardor
glitters with equal brilliance, at one and the same time,
in the inexpressible Relationship that is being set up
between me and you:
Jesus!

ANTIPHON

Without earthquake, or thunderclap:
the flame has lit up the whole world from within.

NIGHT PSALM

Once again the Fire has penetrated the earth.
Not with sudden crash of thunderbolt,
riving the mountain-tops:
does the Master break down doors to enter their own home?

Without earthquake, or thunderclap:
the flame has lit up the whole world from within.

All things individually and collectively
are penetrated and flooded by it,
from the inmost core of the tiniest atom
to the mighty sweep of the most universal laws of being.

So naturally has it flooded every element, every energy,
every connecting link in the unity of our cosmos,

that one might suppose the cosmos
to have burst spontaneously into flame.

Word prolongs the unending act of being born.
Through Your own incarnation, my God,
all matter is henceforth incarnate.

Psalm Prayer

Christ guides from within the universal progress
of the world.
May our consciousness
of the bond that runs through all things,
of their constant movement in being, grow ever more keen,
and so make the impact of Christ upon us ever greater.

~Silence~

Litany

Jesus, Savior of human activity
to which you have given meaning,
Jesus, Savior of human suffering
to which you have given living value,
Jesus, be also the Savior of human unity.
Compel us to discard our pettiness and venture forth,
resting upon you, into the uncharted ocean of charity.

CLOSING PRAYER

In the guise of a tiny babe in its mother's arms,
obeying the great law of birth,
You came, Lord Jesus, to swell in my infant soul.

Your humanity which once was born and dwelt in Palestine
spread out gradually everywhere
like an iridescence of unnumbered hues.

Without destroying anything,
your presence penetrated and endued with super vitality
every other presence about me.

Tuesday

Living Earth

Dawn

Rich with the sap of the world,
I rise up towards the Spirit.

INVOCATION

Let us awaken to the light: the world is full of God!
For if it were empty,
the world would long ago have died of disgust.

DOXOLOGY

I bless you, matter, and you I acclaim
as you reveal yourself to me today,
in your totality and your true nature.

Opening Verse

There is a communion with God,
and a communion with earth,
and a communion with God through earth.

Hymn

Blazing Spirit,
Fire, personal, super-substantial,
the consummation of a union
immeasurably more lovely and more desirable
than that destructive fusion of which all the pantheists dream.

Be pleased yet once again
to come down and breathe a soul
into the newly formed, fragile film of matter
with which this day the world is to be freshly clothed.

Antiphon

The living surface of the earth wakes and trembles.

Psalm

Over there, on the horizon,
the sun has just touched with light
the outermost fringe of the eastern sky.

Once again, beneath this moving sheet of fire,
the living surface of the earth
wakes and trembles,
and once again begins its fearful travail.

Once again, I will place on my paten, O God,
the harvest to be won by this renewal of labor.

Antiphon

The earth has a face.
We are just beginning to decipher its features.

Psalm

The earth has a face.
Having made the circuit of our universe,
we are just beginning to decipher its features.

Patiently assembled,
the innumerable details gathered about the earth's surface
are beginning to fit together.
They are gaining meaning for our eyes.

Soon it will be no more permissible
to be ignorant that the earth has a face, an expression,
than not to know that it is round and revolves.

Oceans, continents, mountains.
Have not these monotonous features of our globe,
these brown or blue hatchings or expanses,
begun to assume for us a sort of life and shape?

How can we express the appearance
which their face now takes in our eyes?

Psalm Prayer

Pantheized: no longer to adhere vitally to God
through some central and specially favored point
of our being,
but to communicate, to *super-communicate*, with God
without fusion or confusion
through all the height, the breadth, the depths
and the multiplicity
of the organic powers of space and time.
For as love unites its terms,
so it differentiates and personalizes them.

Reading

Some thousands of millions of years ago, as the result of some
unbelievable accident—a brush with another star? an internal
upheaval?—a fragment of matter composed of particularly
stable atoms was detached from the surface of the sun. Without
breaking the bonds attaching it to the rest, and just at the right
distance from the mother-star to receive a moderate radiation,
this fragment began to condense, to roll itself up, to take shape.

Containing within its globe and orbit the future of humanity, another heavenly body—a planet this time—had been born. It is the only place in the world in which we are so far able to study the evolution of matter in its ultimate phases, and as far as ourselves.

On the earth this simplicity of the elements still obtains at the periphery, in the more or less ionized gases of the atmosphere and the stratosphere, and in the metals of the barysphere. But between these two extremes comes a long series of complex substances, harbored and produced only by stars that have gone out. Arranged in successive zones, they demonstrate from the start the powers of synthesis contained in the universe.

First the siliceous zone, preparing the solid crust of the planet. Next the zone of water and carbonic acid, enclosing the silicates in an unstable, mobile and penetrating envelope. In other words, we have the barysphere, lithosphere, hydrosphere, atmosphere and stratosphere.

VERSICLE

God bent over the now intelligent mirror of earth
to impress on it the first marks of His beauty.

~SILENCE~

RESPONSORY

To be pure of heart means to love God above all things
and at the same time to see God everywhere in all things.

Cosmic Canticle

Hymn to Matter

Blessed be you,
harsh matter, barren soil, stubborn rock—
you who yield only to violence,
you who force us to work if we would eat.

Blessed be you,
perilous matter, violent sea, untamable passion—
you who unless we fetter you, will devour us.

Blessed be you,
mighty matter, irresistible march of evolution,
reality ever newborn—
you who by constantly shattering our mental categories
force us to go ever further and further
in our pursuit of the truth.

~Intercessions~

Lord's Prayer

Lord of my childhood and Lord of my last days,
God, complete in Yourself
yet, for us, continually being born,
God, You offer Yourself to our worship as *evolver and evolving,*
the only being that can satisfy us.

Sweep away at last the clouds that still hide You,
the clouds of hostile prejudice and of false creeds.

You have become for my mind and heart
much more than God who was and who is:
You have become God who shall be.

CLOSING PRAYER

Once again, Lord,
I ask which is the most precious of these two beatitudes:
that all things for me should be a contact with You?
Or that You should be so universal
that I can undergo You and grasp You in every creature?

Day

*An animal absorbed in its actions,
never leaves the present moment.*

INVOCATION

O God! Grant to me always to hear and to make others hear,
the music of all things so vividly
that we are swept away in rapture.

DOXOLOGY

I bless you, matter, and you I acclaim
as you reveal yourself to me today,
in your totality and your true nature.

Exhortation

Just trust Life:
A great charm, if only one is convinced
that the world is going somewhere.
It is so easy to be pessimistic or cynical,
about the present and the future of Earth.
Just trust Life:
If I can do it, my life will be full and fulfilled—
people need some constructive hope.

Antiphon

Look upward to the wide areas that wait for new creations!

Psalm

Those whose eyes have been opened
will make their way back into the sealed depths of Nature.

There they will peer down into the vast tangle of branches
that supports them
and disappear into the far distance below them,
lost in the heart of the dim Past.

And once again they will fill their souls to overflowing
as they contemplate and vibrate in sympathy
with a single-minded and determined movement

which is written into the series of dead layers
and the present distribution of all living beings.

If they then look upwards,
to the wide areas that wait for new creations,
they will consecrate themselves, body and soul,
with newly strengthened faith,
to a Progress which draws or sweeps along
even those who reject it.

Psalm Prayer

I thank You, my God,
for having in a thousand different ways
led my eyes to discover the immense simplicity of things.

When the World is left to itself
it does not fall in the direction of obscurity;
its vastness and all its weight fall forward in equilibrium,
towards the light.

Meditation

I have contemplated nature for so long and have so loved her
countenance, recognized unmistakably as hers, that I now have
a deep conviction, dear to me, infinitely precious and unshak-
able, the humblest and yet the most fundamental in the whole
structure of my convictions, that life is never mistaken, either
about its road or its destination.

Prayer

Let us pray: Lord Jesus Christ,
You truly contain within Your gentleness,
within Your humanity,
all the unyielding immensity and grandeur of the world.
And it is because of this, my heart,
enamored of cosmic reality,
gives itself passionately to You.

~Reflection~

Lesson

The fact is that creation has never stopped. The creative act is one huge continual gesture, drawn out over the totality of time. It is still going on; and, incessantly even if imperceptibly, the world is constantly emerging a little farther above nothing-ness. Through the whole breadth and depth of the cosmos, it is in truth the divine action that still molds us, as it molded the clay on the first day of creation.

Collect

Without leaving the world, plunge into God.
There, and from there, in God and through God,
we shall hold all things.

Examen

Learn not to stifle the spirit of earth in us. But let there be no mistake. They who wish to share in this spirit must die and be reborn, to themselves and to others. To reach this higher plane of humanity, they must not only reflect and see a particular situation intellectually, but make a complete change in their fundamental way of valuation and action. In them, a new plane (individual, social and religious) must eliminate another. This entails inner tortures and persecutions. The earth will only become conscious of itself through the crisis of conversion.

Kyrie

Let us hope that the passion for unity blazes up in us
    with more ardor than the passion for destruction
    that is ranged against us. *Kyrie Eleison*
Love one another. This gentle precept,
    which two thousand years ago came like a soothing oil
    humbly poured on human suffering,
    offers itself to our modern spirit. *Christe Eleison*
Love is the only synthesizing energy whose differentiating
    action can super-personalize us. *Kyrie Eleison*

Benediction

Let the silent peace of your native mountains enter into you
    and live in you.

You need this rest if you are to take up again the activities
    that call you and await you, so that they may sanctify you.

Nature is a penetrating summons to the slow efforts,
patient and unseen,
by which the individual,
borne along by a whole past,
humbly prepares a world they will never know.

Dusk

Plunge into the midst of created things.

Invocation

O wonder-laden Center! O immense sphere! O God!

Doxology

I bless you, matter, and you I acclaim
as you reveal yourself to me today,
in your totality and your true nature.

Opening Verse

Love as energy.
Driven by the forces of love, the fragments of the world

seek each other so that the world may come to being.
This is no metaphor; and it is much more than poetry.

Evening Hymn

Like a huge fire
that is fed by what should normally extinguish it,
or like a mighty torrent which is swelled
by the very obstacles placed to stem it,
so the tension engendered by the encounter
between humanity and God
dissolves, bears along and volatilizes created things
and makes them all, equally, serve the cause of union.

Joys, advances, sufferings,
setbacks, mistakes, works,
prayers, beauties, the powers of heaven, earth and hell,
everything bows down
under the touch of the heavenly waves;

and everything yields up the portion of positive energy
contained within its nature
so as to contribute to the richness of the *divine milieu*.

Antiphon

Faith and hope in the terrestrial World
have come to dominate my inner life
like great mountains.

73

PSALM

Picture an immense basaltic plateau,
averaging eighteen hundred meters in height,
covered with vast meadows,
without a living soul,
and here and there in the ravines or on the ridges,
bits of forest land: fir, larch, birch.

In this rugged country the flowering season
is sudden and opulent.

Everywhere there were carpets of yellow and red lilies,
dwarf or tall iris, tall scarlet primroses,
large white peonies, rhubarb with cream-colored tufts,
silver, violet, or turquoise blue flowers.

In the moist lowlands,
orchids (lady's slippers) flaunted calyxes as fat as walnuts.

It was enchanting in its life, spaciousness, and solitude.

Faith and hope in the terrestrial World
have come to dominate my inner life like great mountains.

ANTIPHON

Heaven does not stand in opposition to earth:
it is born from the transformation of earth.

74

Psalm

The divine light
does not appear in the night
artificially created inside ourselves;
like a supreme and inextinguishable glow,
it plays over the organic shimmer of the world.

The fundamental note of the cosmos
cannot be heard in absolute silence;
it rises over the harmony of elementary vibrations.

Heaven does not stand in opposition to earth:
it is born from the transformation of earth.
God is reached, not by a draining away of self,
but by sublimation.

Such is the great religious discovery of the new age.

Psalm Prayer

Take up in Your hands, Lord, and bless this universe that is destined to sustain and fulfill the plenitude of Your being among us. Make this universe ready to be united with You: and that this may be so, intensify the magnetism that comes down from Your heart to draw to it the dust of which we are made.

Epistle

Since all time, the poets—the true poets—have felt the presence of the soul of the world, in the solitude of the deserts, in nature's fruitful breath, in the fathomless swell of the human heart. Everywhere it asserted itself as a living thing, and yet nowhere could they grasp it; and their loftiest inspiration was but the distress they suffered from its elusive presence. Throughout the centuries the soul of the world has constantly, from the manifold energy exerted by its magnetism, provided fuel for human enthusiasm and passion in their most intense form.

~Silence~

Responsory

Everything becomes animate and fit for love and worship.

Cosmic Canticle

Hymn to Matter

Blessed be you, universal matter—
immeasurable time, boundless ether,
triple abyss of stars and atoms and generations:
you who by overflowing and dissolving
our narrow standards or measurement
reveal to us the dimensions of God.

Blessed be you, impenetrable matter—
you who interposed between our minds
and the world of essences,
cause us to languish with the desire
to pierce through the seamless veil of phenomena.

Blessed be you, mortal matter—
you who one day will undergo
the process of dissolution within us
and will thereby take us forcibly
into the very heart of that which exists.

I bless you, matter, and you I acclaim
as you reveal yourself to me today,
in your totality and your true nature.

~Intercessions~

Lord's Prayer

Lord of my childhood and Lord of my last days,
God, complete in Yourself
yet, for us, continually being born,
God, You offer Yourself to our worship as *evolver and evolving,*
the only being that can satisfy us.

Sweep away at last the clouds that still hide You,
the clouds of hostile prejudice and of false creeds.

You have become for my mind and heart
much more than God who was and who is:
You have become God who shall be.

Closing Prayer

My dearest wish, Master,
is that I might offer so little resistance to You
that You could no longer distinguish me from Yourself—
so perfectly would we be united, in a communion of will.

Dark

At the heart of Matter
A World-heart
the Heart of a God.

Invocation

Sense of Plenitude,
Sense of Consummation and of Completion!
The *Pleromic* Sense, the Stuff of Things.

Doxology

I bless you, matter, and you I acclaim
as you reveal yourself to me today,
in your totality and your true nature.

Opening Verse

Something is growing, most evidently,
in the spiritual atmosphere of the world.

Night Hymn

Everything that is active, that moves or breathes,
every physical, astral, or animate energy,
every fragment of force, every spark of life,
is equally sacred.

For, in the humblest atom
and the most brilliant star,
in the lowest insect
and the finest intelligence,
there is the radiant smile and thrill
of the same Absolute.

Antiphon

In our universe, everything is born.
Everything, including the All.

Night Psalm

Once upon a time everything seemed fixed and solid.
Now everything in the universe
has begun to slide under our feet:
mountains, continents, life, and even matter itself.

If we look at it from a sufficient height,
we no longer see the world revolving,
but a new world
gradually changing color, shape and even consciousness.
No longer the cosmos, but *cosmogenesis.*

A process is not a philosophical explanation.
In our empirical universe, everything is born,
everything establishes itself and grows by successive phases.

Everything, including the All.

ANTIPHON

Life swarms and hovers.

NIGHT PSALM

Air and sea:
a thick, living envelope,
in which life swarms and hovers,
as fluid and dense as the medium that holds it.

Astonishment before the shape and the wonderful flight
of the gull: how was that craft built?

The worst failing of our minds
is that we fail to see the really big problems
simply because the forms in which they arise
are right under our eyes.

How many gulls have I seen,
how many other people have seen them,
without giving a thought
to the mystery that accompanies their flight?

PSALM PRAYER

Mighty nature is at work for us;
she has made it her business to look to the future,
to be the guide, to make the decisions,
and all we have to do is to surrender ourselves
to her guidance.

~SILENCE~

LITANY

You the Center at which all things meet
and which stretches out over all things
so as to draw them back into itself:

I love You, Lord Jesus,
because of the multitude who shelter within You
and in whom, if one clings closely to You,
one can hear with all the other beings
murmuring, praying, weeping.

I love You as the source,
the activating and lifegiving ambience,

the term and consummation of the world,
even of the natural world, and of its process of becoming.

I love You for the extensions of Your body and soul
to the farthest corners of creation
through grace, through life, and through matter.

Closing Prayer

Lord Jesus, You who are as gentle as the human heart,
as fiery as the forces of nature, as intimate as life itself,
You in whom I can melt away
and with whom I must have mastery and freedom:
I love You as a world,
as this world which has captivated my heart.
And it is You, I now realize, that my fellow human kin,
even those who do not believe,
sense and seek throughout the magic immensities
of the cosmos.

Becoming Human

Dawn

*In us the world's evolution towards spirit
has become conscious.*

INVOCATION

Radiant Word, blazing Power!
You mold the manifold so as to breathe Your life into it.

DOXOLOGY

At this very moment,
by everything we do,
we all share in all,
through and in Christ,
the spirit of the earth.

Opening Verse

Only one thing concerns me,
only one thing guides me:
to try to be as true as possible to Life.

Hymn

Like a rising tide,
the mystical milieu has pursued its task
of entering into and refashioning the Real.

I realize that the mystical effort to see
must give way to the effort to feel
and to surrender myself.

This is the phase of communion.

Gladly, then, I welcome each in its due order
and according to its own measure:

every force and every charm,
every form and every movement,
everything that is great and strong,
everything that stands and endures,
everything that reaches out,
and overflows its own limits.

Antiphon

A flame bursts forth: thought is born.

Psalm

We see the tree of life standing before us.
A strange tree, no doubt.

Life is the rise of consciousness.
If it is to progress still further it can only be
because the internal energy is secretly rising up
under the mantle of the flowering earth.

But in one well-marked region at the heart of the mammals,
where the most powerful brains
ever made by nature are to be found,
they become red hot.

And right at the heart of that glow
burns a point of incandescence.

We must not lose sight of that line crimsoned by the dawn:
after thousands of years rising below the horizon,
a flame bursts forth at a strictly localized point.
Thought is born.

Antiphon

Discover the secret of the real.

Psalm

What we seek throughout our lives,
what we strive for more than for our daily bread
and any material well-being,
is knowledge.

The very essence of our life
is our urge not for a better life,
but for a fuller degree of life.

Deeply rooted in the minds of all of us
is the conviction that a mysterious fire
lies hidden somewhere around us,
and that if we are to be happy
we must get possession of it as a torch
to shed light on our understanding
of the profound significance of the world.

By investigating nature,
we shall be able to discover the secret of the real,
put our hand on the underlying forces
that control the growth of beings
that we may read the secret, track down the source.

And scientific research, for all its claim to be positivist,
is colored and haloed—or rather is irresistibly animated—
by a mystical hope.

Thus the essential urge of our mind
is to try to penetrate
to the heart of the world.

Psalm Prayer

Lord, that I might hold You more closely,
I would that my consciousness were
as wide as the skies and the earth
and the peoples of the earth;
as deep as the past, the desert, the ocean;
as tenuous as the atoms of matter
or the thoughts of the human heart.

Reading

No, the cosmos could not possibly be explained as a dust of
unconscious elements, on which life, for some incomprehensible reason, burst into flower—as an accident or as a mold.
But it is *fundamentally and primarily* living, and its complete
history is ultimately an immense psychic exercise; the slow but
progressive attaining of a diffused consciousness—a gradual
escape from the *material* conditions which *secondarily* veil it in
an initial state of extreme plurality.

From this point of view, the human is nothing but the point

of emergence in nature, at which this deep cosmic evolution culminates and declares itself. From this point onwards the human ceases to be a spark fallen by chance on earth and coming from another place.

Humanity is the flame of a general fermentation of the universe which breaks out suddenly on the earth. Humanity is no longer a sterile enigma or discordant note in nature.

Humanity is the key of things and the final harmony. In the human everything takes shape and is explained.

Versicle

Humanity is the collective subject of a real evolution!

~Silence~

Responsory

The sense of evolution, the sense of species,
the sense of the earth, the sense of the human.

Cosmic Canticle

We are called by the music of the universe
to reply, each with our own pure and incommunicable
   harmonic.

As love for the All advances in our hearts,
we feel stretching out beyond the diversity

of our efforts and desires
the bounding simplicity of an urge
in which the innumerable shades of passion and action
mingle in exaltation without ever becoming confused.

Then, within the mass formed by human energy,
we shall each approach the plenitude of our powers and
    personality.

We are inevitably approaching a new age
in which the world will throw off its chains and at last,
give itself up to the power of its inner affinities.

Either we must doubt the value of everything around us,
or we must utterly believe in the possibility
and in the inevitable consequences,
of universal love.

~Intercessions~

Lord's Prayer

Lord of my childhood and Lord of my last days,
God, complete in Yourself
yet, for us, continually being born,
God, You offer Yourself to our worship as *evolver and evolving,*
the only being that can satisfy us.

Sweep away at last the clouds that still hide You,
the clouds of hostile prejudice and of false creeds.

You have become for my mind and heart
much more than God who was and who is:
You have become God who shall be.

CLOSING PRAYER

Not in the form of a ray of light but as fire I desire You;
and it was as fire I felt Your presence,
in the intuition of my first contact.

I shall never find rest,
unless some active force pours down from You,
to cover and transform me.

Day

*The glorious responsibility and splendid ambition
that is ours: fashioning our own self.*

INVOCATION

Radiant Word, blazing Power!
Lay on us Your hands.

DOXOLOGY

At this very moment,
by everything we do,
we all share in all,
through and in Christ,
the spirit of the earth.

Exhortation

We are not simply nurslings
rocked and suckled by Mother Earth.
Like children who have grown up,
we must learn to walk by ourselves
and give active help to the mother who bore us.

Antiphon

Inextinguishable fire is radiant within me.

Psalm

An inextinguishable Core of fire
is radiant within me,
and in this all my activity finds warmth:
the vast, intimate, single World.

In its heat the passion for the universal Real
is kept alive deep down in my being.

Human action seems
to be completely satisfying and conscious
only when it is carried through
in union with the fulfilment of all cosmic perfection.

Psalm Prayer

What I desire so greatly is a certain taste, a certain perception of the beauty, the pathos, and the unity of being.

Meditation

Reflection is, as the word indicates, the power acquired by a consciousness to turn in upon itself, to take possession of itself as of an object endowed with its own particular consistence and value: no longer merely to know, but to know oneself; no longer merely to know, but to know that one knows.

The being who is the object of their own reflection, in consequence of that very doubling back upon themself, becomes in a flash able to rise into a new sphere. In reality, another world is born. Abstraction, logic, reasoned choice and inventions, mathematics, art, calculation of space and time, anxieties and dreams of love—all these activities of inner life are nothing else than the effervescence of the newly-formed center as it explodes onto itself. Admittedly the animal knows. But it cannot know that it knows: that is quite certain.

Prayer

Lord, lock me up in the deepest depths of Your heart; and then, holding me there, burn me, purify me, set me on fire, sublimate me, till I become utterly what You would have me be, through the utter annihilation of my ego.

Lesson

The consciousness that we see filling the avenues of the past does not flow simply like a river which carries an unchanging water past ever changing banks. It transforms itself in the course of its journey; it evolves; life has a movement of its own. If we follow it backwards in time, we see it reducing the organic complexity of its forms and the range of its spontaneity. Nervous systems become increasingly rudimentary. And to judge from the present survivors of these ancient stages, the animate world disappears at the farthest end into a swarm of living particles that are hardly separate from molecular energies.

Inversely, in the direction of the arrow of time, cellular constructions are formed and, step by step with a growth in complexity, consciousness increases its powers of internal clairvoyance and interconnexion until, at the level of humanity, reflective thought bursts forth. The phenomenon of spirit is not a sort of brief flash in the night; it reveals a gradual and systematic passage from the unconscious to the conscious, and from the conscious to the self-conscious. It is a cosmic change of state.

Collect

We are more outside ourselves in time and space
than we are inside ourselves, every second of our lives.
The person is essentially cosmic.

Examen

Which of us has ever in our life really had the courage to look squarely at and try to *live* a universe formed of galaxies whose distance apart runs into hundreds of thousands of light years? Which of us, having tried, has not emerged from the ordeal shaken in one or other of our beliefs?

And who, even when trying to shut our eyes as best we can to what the astronomers implacably put before us, has not had a confused sensation of a gigantic shadow passing over the serenity of our joy?

Like children who have grown up, like workers who have become *conscious*, we are discovering that something is developing in the world by means of us, perhaps at our expense.

And what is more serious still is that we have become aware that, in the great game that is being played, we are the players as well as being the cards and the stakes.

Kyrie

What is imponderable in the world
    is greater than what we can handle. *Kyrie Eleison*
What radiates from living beings
    is more valuable than their caresses. *Christe Eleison*
What has not yet come
    is more precious than what is already born. *Kyrie Eleison*

BENEDICTION

Grant, O God, that the light of Your countenance
may shine for me in the life of others.
The irresistible light of Your eyes
shining in the depth of things
has already guided me
towards all the work I must accomplish,
and all the difficulties I must pass through.
Grant that I may see You, even and above all,
in the souls of all my kin, at their most personal,
and most true, and most distant.

Dusk

*It is better, no matter what the cost, to be
more conscious than less conscious.*

Invocation

Radiant Word, blazing Power!
Reach us simultaneously
through all that is most immense and most inward
within us and around us.

Doxology

At this very moment,
by everything we do,
we all share in all,
through and in Christ,
the spirit of the earth.

Opening Verse

Thought would not be queen of the world
if it were not connected with the world
by all the fibers of matter, even the most humble ones.

Evening Hymn

Poet, philosopher, mystic—
it is hardly possible to be one
without being the others.

In the great stream of past humankind,
poets, philosophers, and mystics—
the long procession of those who have been initiated
into the vision and cult of the Whole—
have left behind them a central wake
which we can follow unmistakably from our own days
right back to the most distant horizons of history.

In one sense, therefore, we may say
that a concern for the Whole is extremely ancient.
It belongs to all ages.

Antiphon

Each grain of thought, specific to the earth:
a spirit of the earth.

PSALM

The idea of the electron or the quantum, or the cosmic ray—
the idea of the cell or of heredity—
the idea of humanity or even the idea of God—
no single individual can claim these
as their own preserve or dominate them.

The quantity of activity and consciousness
contained in humankind, taken as a whole,
is greater than the mere sum
of individual activity and consciousness.

Progress in complexity is making itself felt
in a deepening of centricity.
It is not simply a sum, but synthesis.

Each grain of thought,
now taken to the extreme limit
of its individual consciousness,
will simply be the incommunicable,
partial, elementary expression
of a total consciousness
which is common to the whole earth,
and specific to the earth: a spirit of the earth.

ANTIPHON

Millions of Milky Ways whirl in space.

Psalm

The stellar universe is not centered on the earth,
and terrestrial life is not centered on humankind.

The movement which carries us along takes the form
not of a divergence from a lower cosmic center,
but rather of a slow concentration,
from layers of extreme diffusion.

Even if an initial center of the world does exist,
we certainly cannot locate it among human beings.

Thousands of centuries
before a thinking being appeared on our earth,
life swarmed on it,
with its instincts and its passions,
its sufferings and its deaths.

And it is almost impossible to conceive
that, among the millions of Milky Ways which whirl in space,
there is not one which has known, or is going to know,
conscious life.

Psalm Prayer

Tell me, O thinking World,
gravitating in the spiritual void,
laden with the soul of all peoples,

what force keeps you consolidated upon yourself?
And what pull, checking your fall, acts as your guide?

Epistle

So I've been able to think over at leisure what you say about the difficulties you find in "living in the world as though not being of the world." This is what I have to say.

Above all, trust in the slow work of God. We are, quite naturally, impatient in everything to reach the end without delay. We should like to skip the intermediate stages. We are impatient of being on the way to something unknown, something new. And yet it is the law of all progress that it is made by passing through some stages of instability—and that may take a very long time.

Thus, we have been through a whole year's suspense, not knowing what the future holds for civilization. And so, I think, it is with you. Your ideas mature gradually—let them grow, let them shape themselves, without undue haste. Don't try to *force* them on, as though you could be today what time (that is to say, grace and circumstances acting on your own good will) will make you tomorrow.

Only God could say what this new spirit gradually forming within you will be. Give our Lord the benefit of believing that the hand of God is leading you surely through the obscurity and the *becoming*, and accept, for love of God, the anxiety of feeling yourself in suspense and incomplete.

~Silence~

Responsory

The very expansion of our energy
is our obedience to a will to be and to grow.

Cosmic Canticle

The world glows with a new warmth:
that is to say, it opens wholly to the power of Love.

To love is to discover and complete one's self
in someone other than oneself,
an act impossible of general realization on earth
so long as each can see in their neighbor
no more than a closed fragment
following its own course through the world.

It is precisely this state of isolation that will end
if we begin to discover in each other
not merely the elements of one and the same thing,
but of a single Spirit in search of itself.

Because we love,
and in order that we may love even more,
we find ourselves happily and especially compelled
to participate in all the endeavors, all the anxieties,
all the aspirations, and also all the affections of the earth—
in so far as these embody a principle
of ascension and synthesis.

106

LORD'S PRAYER

Lord of my childhood and Lord of my last days,
God, complete in Yourself
yet, for us, continually being born,
God, You offer Yourself to our worship as *evolver and evolving,*
the only being that can satisfy us.

Sweep away at last the clouds that still hide You,
the clouds of hostile prejudice and of false creeds.

You have become for my mind and heart
much more than God who was and who is:
You have become God who shall be.

CLOSING PRAYER

Through everything in me that has subsistence and resonance,
everything that enlarges me from within,
everything that arouses me, attracts me,
wounds me from without:
through all these, Lord, You work upon me,
You mold and spiritualize my formless clay,
You transform me into Yourself.

Dark

*All conscious energy is, like love (and because it is love),
founded on hope.*

INVOCATION

Radiant Word, blazing Power, considerate, omnipresent!
Plunge into the depths and the totality of things.

DOXOLOGY

At this very moment,
by everything we do,
we all share in all,
through and in Christ,
the spirit of the earth.

OPENING VERSE

The moon herself feels the pull and the heat of the stars
in whose company she moves.
But what friendly thought
will be able to find its way through space
as far as us?

NIGHT HYMN

Love is the most universal,
the most tremendous
and the most mysterious of the cosmic forces.

Huge, ubiquitous and always unsubdued—
this wild force seems to have defeated
all hopes of understanding and governing it.

It is therefore allowed
to run everywhere beneath our civilization.

We are conscious of it,
but all we ask of it is to amuse us,
or not to harm us.

Is it truly possible for humanity to continue
to live and grow without asking itself
how much truth and energy it is losing
by neglecting its incredible power of love?

ANTIPHON

What is rising up this evening?

NIGHT PSALM

From a stretcher-bearer in time of war

I have just seen the moon rise over the ridge.
The slim, hesitant crescent of the last few twilights
has gradually turned into a full, luminous disc.

The moon,
invisible a fortnight ago,
detaches herself,
unique and glorious, from the black earthen parapets;
she seems to be gliding through the barbed wire.

On these uplands,
the scene of our conflicts, on these flats,
hardly different from what they are now,
there was a time when no human yet trod.

There were only herds of ruminants
to animate the solitude in which thought did not exist—
in which nothing stable was taking shape.

And then one day,
after the horses, the antelopes, the elephants—

110

hunting the wild animals of the open country
and hunted themselves by life,
thinking beings appeared here,
coming from somewhere in the East.

The instinct for discovery,
the need for space,
flight from the stronger—
these drove them on,
until their flood came up against the sea's flood.
It was through these wandering hunters
that Humankind was stretching the first threads
of its network over the face of the Earth.

My heart was trembling with an emotion
that embraced everything in the world,
when, over the torn and blackened earth,
there rose the great Monad.

What is rising up this evening
from the dimly outlined trenches to my front?
Is it the Moon, or is it rather the Earth,
a unified Earth, a new Earth?

ANTIPHON

Humanity is an immense cosmic energy.

Night Psalm

The mass of humanity
is also a magnificent element.
But ordinarily we perceive only the atoms, the individuals,
and as a result, its grandeur escapes us.

I find that the sea, the mountains, the Milky Way,
reveal and enhance Humanity as an immense cosmic energy;

and it seems to me that this grandeur,
far from overpowering the individual,
imparts an inexhaustible charm and mystery.

Psalm Prayer

Lord Jesus,
now that beneath the world forces
You have become truly and physically
everything for me,
everything about me,
everything within me,
I shall gather into a single prayer
both my delight in what I have
and my thirst for what I lack.

~Silence~

Litany

Every being in our universe is by its material organization
part and parcel of a whole past.
So, as far as the eye can see,
living strata succeed one another,
living creatures replace one another,
develop and ramify according to the same rhythm.
And in this harmony the silences themselves
have their precise significance.

Australopithecines
Pithecanthropus
Sinanthropus
Homo Rhodesian
Homo Neanderthal
Javanthropus
Homo Sapiens

With Homo Sapiens
we leave the half-dark of humankind's infancy
to attain a clear vision of the human phenomenon.

Closing Prayer

O God,
whose call precedes the very first of our movements,
grant me the desire to desire being—

that, by means of that divine thirst which is Your gift,
the access to the great waters may open wide within me.

Do not deprive me of the sacred taste for being,
that primordial energy,
that very first of our points of rest.

Thursday

Building the World

Dawn

O you who are matter: my heart is trembling.
Tell me: what would you have me do?

INVOCATION

How strange, my God, are the processes Your Spirit initiates!

DOXOLOGY

Oh, the beauty of spirit as it rises up
adorned with all the riches of the earth!

OPENING VERSE

The tempest of life, infinitely gentle, infinitely brutal,
was murmuring in the soul:

You called me: here I am.
You had need of me in order to grow;
and I was waiting for You in order to be made holy.
Always You have, without knowing it, desired me;
and always I have been drawing You to me.

HYMN

God, in all that is most living and incarnate,
You are not far away from us,
altogether apart from the world we see,
touch, hear, smell and taste about us.

Rather You await us every instant
in our action,
in the work of the moment.

There is a sense in which
You are at the tip of my pen, my spade,
my brush, my needle—
of my heart and of my thought.

By pressing the stroke,
the line, or the stitch,
on which I am engaged,
to its ultimate natural finish,
I shall lay hold of that last end
towards which my innermost will tends.

ANTIPHON

Something is afoot in the universe.

PSALM

The world is under construction.
Through the centuries, a general plan
appears to be in course of realization around us.

Something is afoot in the universe,
a result is working out which can best be compared
to a gestation and birth:
the birth of a spiritual reality formed by souls
and the matter they draw after them.

Laboriously, by way of human activity and thanks to it,
the new earth is gathering, isolating and purifying itself.

No, we are not like flowers in a bunch,
but the leaves and flowers of a great tree,
on which each appears at its time and place,
according to the demands of the All.

ANTIPHON

The offering You really want is the growth of the world.

Psalm

Once upon a time
humans took into Your temple
the first fruits of their harvests,
the flower of their flocks.

But the offering You really want,
the offering You mysteriously need every day
to appease Your hunger, to slake Your thirst
is nothing less than the growth of the world
borne ever onwards
in the stream of universal becoming.

Psalm Prayer

The highest pleasure must be to pour one's soul
into a living creation:
a novel, music, or better still, into another living soul.

Reading

After the nineteenth century's often childish worship of progress, today, in the light shed by the discovery of time and of energies we have mastered, and of our vision of human unity, we are initiates, and we are beginning to see into ourselves and ahead of ourselves, sharply and clearly.

In earlier days we saw ourselves as passive and irresponsible spectators watching a great terrestrial panorama. We were still children. Today, we have understood that we are workers pledged to a vast enterprise. We feel that we are living atoms in a universe that is under way. We have become adult. We, too, are experiencing a passionate re-birth into the universe.

Versicle

Through and beyond matter, spirit is hard at work, building.
God does not so much *make* things
as *make them make themselves.*

~Silence~

Responsory

Created beings must work if they would be further created.

Cosmic Canticle

This bread, our toil,
is of itself, I know,
but an immense fragmentation;
this wine, our pain,
is no more, I know,
than a draught that dissolves.

Yet in the very depths of this formless mass
You have implanted a desire, irresistible, hallowing,
which makes us cry out,

believer and unbeliever alike:
Lord, make us one!

LORD'S PRAYER

Lord of my childhood and Lord of my last days,
God, complete in Yourself
yet, for us, continually being born,
God, You offer Yourself to our worship as *evolver and evolving,*
the only being that can satisfy us.

Sweep away at last the clouds that still hide You,
the clouds of hostile prejudice and of false creeds.

You have become for my mind and heart
much more than God who was and who is:
You have become God who shall be.

CLOSING PRAYER

The one who is filled with an impassioned love of Jesus
hidden in the forces which bring increase to the earth,
that one the earth will lift up, like a mother,
in the immensity of her arms,
and will enable them to contemplate the face of God.

Day

*Has the curve of my life anything in common
with the fate of the insect scurrying at my feet?*

INVOCATION

I pray you, *divine milieu*!
Show yourself to me as the focus of all energies.

DOXOLOGY

Oh, the beauty of spirit as it rises up
adorned with all the riches of the earth!

EXHORTATION

To understand the world, knowledge is not enough,
you must see it, touch it, live in its presence

and drink the vital heat of existence
in the very heart of reality.

ANTIPHON

The *divine milieu* may be born at any moment.

PSALM

God does not offer Himself to our finite beings
as a thing all complete and ready to be embraced.
For us God is eternal discovery and eternal growth.

The more we think we understand God,
the more God reveals Himself as otherwise.
The more we think we hold God,
the further God withdraws,
drawing us into the depths of Himself.

The nearer we approach God
through all the efforts of nature and grace,
the more God increases His attraction over our powers,
and the receptivity of our powers to that divine attraction.

The one point at which the *divine milieu* may be born,
for each of us, at any moment
is not a fixed point in the universe,
but a moving center which we have to follow,
like the Magi their star.

That star leads each of us differently, by a different path,
in accord with our vocation.
But all the paths which it indicates have this in common:
that they lead always upward.

Psalm Prayer

A new door opening above, a new stage for development.
If each of us can believe that we are working
so that the Universe may be raised,
in us and through us, to a higher level—
then a new spring of energy will well forth
in the heart of Earth's workers.

Meditation

Humankind no longer knows how to occupy their physical powers: but what is more serious, they do not know towards what universal and final end they should direct the driving force of their souls.

The present crisis is a spiritual crisis. Material energy is no longer circulating with sufficient freedom because it is not finding a spirit strong enough to organize and lead its mass; and the spirit is not strong enough because it is continually being dissipated in restless, undisciplined activity.

Humankind today is undecided, and distressed, at the very peak of its power, because it has not defined its spiritual pole. It lacks religion.

Prayer

I pray you, *divine milieu*, make yourself known to me
in your true essence, which is Creative Action.

~Reflection~

Lesson

The world is like a maze before us. Many entrances, but only
one path that leads to the center. Because we approach at the
wrong angle or from the wrong direction nature resists our
efforts to reach it.

Let us make a better choice of our known and unknown
quantities. Let us put our "x" in the proper place, in the material and the plural; let us recognize that evidences of consciousness and freedom are primordial and defy analysis.

Then we find the right order. No more closed doors or blind
alleys. The Ariadne's thread that can guide us through the
universe is the *birth of the spirit*, and the hand from which we
receive it is the faithful recognition of the *human phenomenon*.

Collect

It is through love and within love that we must look for the
deepening of our deepest self, in the life-giving coming together
of humankind. Love is the free and imaginative outpouring of
the spirit over all unexplored paths.

EXAMEN

One early dawn, in the "bad lands" of Arizona, a dazzling flash of light, strangely brilliant in quality, illumined the most distant peaks, eclipsing the first rays of the rising sun.

There followed a prodigious burst of sound. The thing had happened.

For the first time on earth an atomic fire had burned for the space of a second, industriously kindled by the science of Man. But having thus realized his dream of creating a new thunderclap, Man, stunned by his success, looked inward and sought by the glare of the lightning his own hand had loosed, to understand its effect upon himself.

His body was safe; but what had happened to his soul?

Examine, in the case of the atomic bomb, the effects of the invention upon the inventor, arising out of the fact of the invention.

By the liberation of atomic energy on a massive scale, and for the first time, man has not only changed the face of the earth; he has by the very act set in motion at the heart of his being a long chain of reactions which, in the brief flash of an explosion of matter, has made of him, virtually at least, a new being hitherto unknown to himself.

KYRIE

Humankind has just entered into the most extensive period
　　of transformation it has known since its birth. *Kyrie Eleison*

The seat of the evil we are suffering from is to be found
   in the very foundations of thought on earth. *Christe Eleison*
Each of our actions has its deep-seated repercussions
   upon our subsequent inner orientation. *Kyrie Eleison*

BENEDICTION

Bathe yourself in the ocean of matter;
plunge into it where it is deepest and most violent;
struggle in its currents and drink of its waters.
For it cradled you long ago in your preconscious existence;
and it is that ocean that will raise you up to God.

Dusk

The work God does within us is more precious than any success.

INVOCATION

Lord, You penetrate my heart!
Make its life flow out into Yourself.

DOXOLOGY

Oh, the beauty of spirit as it rises up
adorned with all the riches of the earth!

OPENING VERSE

The tempest of life, infinitely gentle, infinitely brutal,
was murmuring in the soul:

I am the fire that consumes and the water that overthrows;
I am the love that initiates and the truth that passes away.
All that compels acceptance and all that brings renewal;
all that breaks apart and all that binds together;
power, experiment, progress—matter: all this am I.

EVENING HYMN

I can think of nothing more appropriate
nor more valuable to offer you
than a few words in praise of unity.

Science, art, politics,
ethics, thought, mysticism:
these are so many different forms
of one and the same impulse
towards the creation of some harmony.

And in that impulse is expressed,
through the medium of our human activities,
the destiny and the very essence of the universe.

Happiness, power, wealth, wisdom, holiness:
these are all synonyms for a victory over the many.

At the heart of every being lies creation's dream of a
principle which will one day give organic form
to its fragmented treasures.
God is unity.

Antiphon

Welcome the wave-flow, the flood, of the sap of humanity.

Psalm

Lift up your head, Jerusalem,
and see the immense multitude
of those who build and those who seek;
see all those who toil
in laboratories, in studios, in factories,
in the deserts and in the vast crucible of human society.
For all the ferment produced by their labors,
in art, in science, in thought,
all is for you.

Therefore, open wide your arms,
open wide your heart,
and like Christ your Lord
welcome the wave-flow, the flood, of the sap of humanity.

Take it to yourself,
for without its baptism
you will wither away for lack of longing
as a flower withers for lack of water.

Preserve it and care for it,
since without your sun
it will go stupidly to waste in sterile shoots.

What has become of the temptations
aroused by a world too vast in its horizons,
too seductive in its beauty?
They no longer exist.

Antiphon

New beauties appear on the human face of the earth.

Psalm

I love irresistibly
all that Your continuous help
enables me to bring each day to reality.

A thought, a material improvement,
a harmony, a unique nuance of human Love,
the enchanting complexity of a smile or a glance,
all these new beauties that appear for the first time,
in me or around me,
on the human face of the earth—
I cherish them like children
and cannot believe that they will die entirely in their flesh.

If I believed that these things were to perish forever,
should I have given them Life?
The more I examine myself,
the more I discover this psychological truth:
that no one lifts their little finger to do the smallest task

unless moved, however obscurely,
by the conviction that they are contributing infinitesimally
to the building of something definitive—
that is to say, to Your work, my God.

And that being so,
everything which diminishes my explicit faith
in the heavenly value of the results of my endeavor,
diminishes irremediably my power to act.

Psalm Prayer

Show all Your faithful, Lord,
in what a full and true sense
their work follows them into Your realm.
Otherwise they will become like those idle workers
who are not spurred by their task.

Epistle

The smaller you feel you are, the better will you adore, for you will be speaking from the inmost depths of your heart; and the better you adore, the more will God enter into your imperfections and make use of you, poor though you may be, to allow much good to radiate from you. You are distressed at seeing the growth of virtue around you, while you yourself make no progress. Humble yourself, pray, implore, but don't worry. The great thing is not that the most saintly soul, the most loved and privileged soul, should be me. All the better, if there is great love for our Lord around: my sole ideal is to be the servant who seeks only to be faithful. Deep down in your soul, set above all things, immovably, as the basis of all your activity, as the criterion of the value and truth of the thoughts that invade your mind, the Peace of God. Everything that contracts you and disturbs you is false—in the name of the laws of Life, in the name of the promises of God.

~Silence~

Responsory

We must preach and practice the Gospel of human Effort.

Cosmic Canticle

God is vibrant in the ether;
and through the ether
makes way into the very marrow
of my material substance.

God is at work within life.
God helps it, raises it up,
gives it the impulse that drives it along,
the appetite that attracts it,
the growth that transforms it.

I can feel God, touch God, live God
in the deep biological current
that runs through my soul and carries it with it.

God shines through and is personified in humankind.
It is God to whom I lend a hand
in the person of my neighbor;
it is God's voice I hear when orders come to me
from those who have authority over me—
and again, as though in a further zone of matter,
I meet and am subject to the dominating
and penetrating contact of God's hand
at the higher level of collective and social energies.

~Intercessions~

Lord's Prayer

Lord of my childhood and Lord of my last days,
God, complete in Yourself
yet, for us, continually being born,
God, You offer Yourself to our worship as *evolver and evolving,*
the only being that can satisfy us.

Sweep away at last the clouds that still hide You,
the clouds of hostile prejudice and of false creeds.

You have become for my mind and heart
much more than God who was and who is:
You have become God who shall be.

Closing Prayer

Whatever your inner state, have complete trust in our Lord, won't you? The work God does within us is more precious than any success, however conscious we are of it and however satisfying it may be.

Dark

Return to God the Kiss that God is forever offering us across the world.

INVOCATION

Lord, You unfurl Your immensity before my eyes!
Display Yourself to me as Universal Being.

DOXOLOGY

Oh, the beauty of spirit as it rises up
adorned with all the riches of the earth!

OPENING VERSE

Child of earth,
steep yourself in the sea of matter,

bathe in its fiery waters,
for it is the source of your life and your youthfulness.

Night Hymn

In order to take possession of me, my God,
You who are so much more remote in Your immensity
and so much deeper in the intimacy of Your indwelling
than all things else,
You take to Yourself and unite together
the immensity of the world
and the intimate depths of my being:
and I am conscious of bearing deep within me
all the strain and struggle of the universe.

Antiphon

The world will open the arms of God to us.

Night Psalm

Because we have believed intensely
and with a pure heart in the world,
the world will open the arms of God to us.

It is for us to throw ourselves into these arms
so that the *divine milieu*
should close around our lives like a circle.

That gesture of ours will be one of an active response
to our daily task.

Faith consecrates the world.
Fidelity communicates with it.
It is fidelity and fidelity alone
that enables us to welcome
the universal and perpetual overtures
of the *divine milieu*;
through fidelity and fidelity alone
can we return to God
the kiss that God is forever offering us across the world.

ANTIPHON

Take up again the impassioned pursuit of the light.

NIGHT PSALM

One by one, Lord,
I see and I love all those whom You have given me
to sustain and charm my life.

One by one also I number
all those who make up that other beloved family
which has gradually surrounded me,
its unity fashioned out of the most disparate elements,
with affinities of the heart,
of scientific research and of thought.

And again, one by one—more vaguely it is true,
yet all inclusively—
I call before me the whole vast anonymous army
of living humanity;
those who surround me and support me
though I do not know them;
those who come, and those who go.

Above all, I call before me
those who in office, laboratory and factory,
through their vision of truth or despite their error,
truly believe in the progress of earthly reality
and will take up again their impassioned pursuit of the light.

Psalm Prayer

Lord, so close at hand and so concrete,
let me savor You at length,
in all that quickens and all that fills to overflowing,
in all that penetrates and all that envelops—
in sweetness of scent, in light, and love, and space.

~Silence~

Litany

By virtue of the Creation and, still more, of the Incarnation,
nothing here below is profane
for those who know how to see.
On the contrary, everything is sacred.

Try, with God's help,
to perceive the connection—
even physical and natural—
which binds your labor
with the building of the kingdom of heaven.

Try to realize that heaven itself smiles upon you
and, through your works, draws you to itself;
remain with only one feeling,
that of continuing to immerse yourself in God.

If your work is dull or exhausting,
take refuge in the inexhaustible and becalming interest
of progressing in the divine life.

If your work enthralls you,
then allow the spiritual impulse
which matter communicates to you
to enter into your taste for God
whom you know better and desire more
under the veil of God's works.

Never, at any time, whether eating or drinking,
consent to do anything without first of all realizing
its significance and constructive value,
and pursuing it with all your might.

CLOSING PRAYER

O God, that at all times You may find me as You desire me
and where You would have me be,
that You may lay hold on me fully,
both by the Within and the Without of myself,
grant that I may never break this double thread of my life.

Friday

Creative Suffering

Dawn

Seek in utter darkness the dawn of God.

INVOCATION

Lord, with every instinct of my being
and through all the changing fortunes of my life—
it is You whom I have ever sought!

DOXOLOGY

God is eternal Being-in-itself
everywhere in process of formation for us.
God is the heart of everything.

OPENING VERSE

Regard Providence across the ages

as brooding over the world in ceaseless effort
to spare that world its bitter wounds and to bind up its hurts.

HYMN

Human suffering,
the sum total of suffering
poured out at each moment over the whole earth,
is like an immeasurable ocean.

But what makes up this immensity?
Is it blackness, emptiness, barren wastes?
No, indeed: it is potential energy.

A price has to be paid for the struggle.
The earth groans in travail with Christ.
Like a wagon that creaks and grinds,
progress advances painfully, bruised and tearful.

Suffering holds hidden within it, in extreme intensity,
the ascensional force of the world.

ANTIPHON

Everything is capable of becoming good.

Psalm

Like an artist
who is able to make use of a fault or an impurity
in the stone they are sculpting or the bronze they are casting
so as to produce more exquisite lines
or a more beautiful tone,
God, without sparing us the partial deaths,
nor the final death,
which form an essential part of our lives,
transfigures them
by integrating them in a better plan—
provided we lovingly trust in God.

Not only our unavoidable ills
but our faults, even our most deliberate ones,
can be embraced in that transformation,
provided always we repent of them.

Not everything is immediately good to those who seek God;
but everything is capable of becoming good.

Antiphon

Rely for support on divine consistence.

Psalm

The flower I held in my hands withered in my hands.
At the turn of the lane a wall rose up before me.

Suddenly, between the trees
I saw the edge of the forest which I thought had no end.

A flame burnt up the paper
on which my thought was written.
The testing time had come.

But it did not bring the unalleviated sorrow I had expected,
of being pulled up short
by the uncertainties and limitations
of every single particular good.

On the contrary, a glorious, unsuspected joy invaded my soul.

And why was this, Lord, if not because,
in the collapse of those immediate supports
I came so dangerously close to accepting for my life,
I knew with a unique experiential certainty
that I would never again rely for support
on anything save Your own divine consistence.

Psalm Prayer

My God, I deliver myself up with utter abandon
to those fearful forces of dissolution
which, I blindly believe, will this day
cause my narrow ego to be replaced by Your divine presence.

Reading

From a great height, our planet would first of all appear blue from the oxygen that envelops it; then green from the vegetation which covers it; then luminous and ever more luminous—from the thought that grows in intensity on its surface. But at the same time it would appear dark—and ever more dark—from a suffering that, throughout the ages, grows in quantity and poignancy in step with the rise of consciousness.

Consider the total suffering of the whole earth at every moment. If only we were able to gather up this formidable magnitude, to gauge its volume, to weigh, count, analyze it—what an astronomic mass, what a terrifying total! And from physical torture to moral agonies, how subtle a range of shades of misery!

If only, through the medium of some conductivity suddenly established between bodies and souls, all the pain were mixed with all the joy of the world, who can say on which side the balance would settle, on that of pain or that of joy?

Within the vast process of arrangement from which life emerges, every success is paid for by a large percentage of failures. One cannot progress in being without paying a mysterious tribute of tears, blood, and sin. It is hardly surprising, then, if all around us some shadows grow more dense at the same time as the light grows brighter: for, when we see it from this angle, suffering in all its forms and all its degrees is no more than a natural consequence of the movement by which we were brought into being.

VERSICLE

In our souls, as on the sea, storms subside gradually.

~SILENCE~

RESPONSORY

Hold our course toward confidence,
not in the World,
but in the *Heart* of the World.

COSMIC CANTICLE

Vast and innumerable as the dazzling surge of creatures
that are sustained and sur-animated by its ocean,
the *divine milieu,* nevertheless retains the transcendence
that allows it to bring back the elements of the world,
without the least confusion,
within its triumphant and personal unity.

Incomparably near and perceptible—
it presses in upon us through all the forces of the universe—
it nevertheless eludes our grasp so constantly
that we can never seize it here below
except by raising ourselves,
uplifted on its waves,
to the extreme limit of our effort.

Present in and drawing at the inaccessible depth
of each creature,
it withdraws always further,
bearing us along with it
towards the common center of all consummation.

Through it, the touch of matter is a purification,
and chastity flowers as the transfiguration of love.

In it, development culminates in renunciation;
attachment to things yet separates us
from everything disintegrating within them.

Death becomes a resurrection.

~INTERCESSIONS~

LORD'S PRAYER

Lord of my childhood and Lord of my last days,
God, complete in Yourself
yet, for us, continually being born,
God, You offer Yourself to our worship as *evolver and evolving*,
the only being that can satisfy us.

Sweep away at last the clouds that still hide You,
the clouds of hostile prejudice and of false creeds.

You have become for my mind and heart

much more than God who was and who is:
You have become God who shall be.

Closing Prayer

Lord, that no poison may harm me this day,
no death destroy me,
no wine befuddle me,
that in every creature I may discover and sense You,
I beg You: give me faith.

Day

*The world is an immense groping, an immense search,
an immense attack.*

Invocation

My God!
Beneath the lineaments of all that I shall encounter this day,
all that happens to me, all that I achieve,
it is You I desire, You I await.

Doxology

God is eternal Being-in-itself
everywhere in process of formation for us.
God is the heart of everything.

Exhortation

We must do all we can to lessen death and suffering.

Antiphon

What exhilarates us human creatures
is the rapture of being possessed.

Psalm

What is there in suffering
that commits me so deeply to You?
Why, when You stretched out nets to imprison me
should I have thrilled with greater joy
than when You offered me wings?

The only element I hanker after in Your gifts
is the fragrance of Your power over me
and the touch of Your hand upon me.

What exhilarates us human creatures
more than freedom, more than the glory of achievement,
is the joy of finding and surrendering to a beauty
greater than the human,
the rapture of being possessed.

Psalm Prayer

Fold your wings, my soul, those wings you had spread wide
to soar to the terrestrial peaks where the light is most ardent.
It is for you simply to await the descent of the Fire—
supposing it to be willing to take possession of you.

One does not draw near to the Absolute by travelling,
but by ecstasy.

Meditation

Ah, You know it Yourself, Lord, through having borne the
anguish of it as a human: on certain days the world seems a terrifying thing: huge, blind and brutal. It buffets us about, drags
us along, and kills us with complete indifference. Heroically,
it may truly be said, humans have contrived to create a more
or less habitable zone of light and warmth in the midst of the
great, cold, black waters—a zone where people have eyes to
see, hands to help, and hearts to love. But how precarious that
habitation is!

At any moment the vast and horrible thing may break in
through the cracks. The thing which we try hard to forget is
always there, separated from us by a flimsy partition: fire, pes-
tilence, storms, earthquakes, dark moral forces—these callously
sweep away in one moment what we had laboriously built up
and beautified with all our intelligence and all our love.

Since my dignity as a person forbids me to close my eyes to
this—like an animal or a child—that I may not succumb to

155

the temptation to curse the universe and the One who made it, God, teach me to adore it by seeing You concealed within it.

Prayer

To Your sovereign power I swear allegiance:
I surrender myself to You, I take You to myself,
I give You my love.

~Reflection~

Lesson

There is a wonderful compensation by which physical evil, if humbly accepted, conquers moral evil. It purifies the soul, spurs it on and detaches it. Acting as a sacrament acts, it effects a mysterious union between the faithful soul and the suffering Christ.

If undertaken in pliant surrender, the pursuit of Christ in the world culminates logically in an impassioned enfolding, heavy with sorrow, in the arms of the Cross.

Eagerly and whole-heartedly, the soul has offered and surrendered itself to all the great currents of nature.

No work is more effective or brings greater peace
than to gather together, in order to soothe it
and offer it to God,
the suffering of the world;
no attitude allows the soul to expand more freely,

than to open itself, generously and tenderly—
with and in Christ—
to sympathy with all suffering, to cosmic compassion.

COLLECT

O Lord, repeat to me the great liberating words,
the words which at once reveal and operate:
"This is my body."

In truth, the huge and dark thing, the phantom, the storm—
if we want it to be so, is You!
"It is I, do not be afraid."

EXAMEN

The things in our life which terrify us,
the things that threw you yourself into agony in the garden,
are, ultimately, only the species or appearance,
the matter of one and the same sacrament.

We have only to believe.
The more threatening and irreducible reality appears,
the more firmly and desperately must we believe.

Then, little by little, we shall see the universal horror unbend,
and then smile upon us,
and then take us in its more than human arms.

The immense hazard and the immense blindness of the world are only an illusion to those who believe.

KYRIE

The vast and horrible thing may break in through the cracks.
Kyrie Eleison
May I not succumb to the temptation to curse the universe.
Christe Eleison
Teach me to adore it by seeing You concealed within it.
Kyrie Eleison

BENEDICTION

Be happy, dear and precious friend.
The only danger would be to hope too little,
and to trust insufficiently.
If ever you have the impression of any shadow,
just laugh at it.
There is light, and only light, in front of us.

Dusk

No: the work is not yet finished,
nor is it doomed.

INVOCATION

Lord, You whom I have set at the heart of universal matter!
Be a resplendence which shines through all things.

DOXOLOGY

God is eternal Being-in-itself
everywhere in process of formation for us.
God is the heart of everything.

Opening Verse

The only thing that matters in our existence is to live more and more intensely from the inside. And this is possible always and everywhere.

Evening Hymn

If we are ever to possess you,
having taken you rapturously in our arms,
we must then go on
to sublimate you through sorrow.

Raise me up then, matter,
to those heights,
through struggle and separation and death.

Raise me up until, at long last,
it becomes possible for me
to embrace the universe.

Antiphon

Deliver us over to the powers of heaven and earth.

Psalm

Blessed be the disappointments
which snatch the cup from our lips;

blessed be the chains
which force us to go where we would not.

Blessed be relentless time
and the unending thralldom in which it holds us:
the inexorable bondage
of time that goes too slowly and frets our impatience,
of time that goes too quickly and ages us,
of time that never stops, and never returns.

Blessed, above all, be death
and the horror of falling back through death
into the cosmic forces.

At the moment of its coming
a power as strong as the universe
pounces upon our bodies
to grind them to dust and dissolve them,
and an attraction more tremendous
than any material tension
draws our unresisting souls
towards their proper center.

Death causes us to lose our footing completely in ourselves
so as to deliver us over to the powers of heaven and earth.

This is its final terror—
but it is also, for the mystic, the climax of their bliss.

Trust and wait patiently, for all things take time.

PSALM

Do not brace yourself against suffering.
Try to close your eyes and surrender yourself,
as if to a great loving energy.

This attitude is neither weak nor absurd,
it is the only one that cannot lead us astray—
unless life itself is inherently a contradictory and stupid thing,
which its very existence belies.

Trust blindly and wait patiently, for all things take time;
indeed, this is the very reason
for the existence of Time in the World.

Trust and patience:
borne on these two wings,
you have a chance of seeing
the face of a God appear within you.

PSALM PRAYER

Lord, by every innate impulse
and through all the hazards of my life

I have been driven ceaselessly to search for You
and to set You in the heart of the universe of matter.

Epistle

At first I thought that instead of working to improve things in the world, would it not be better to abandon to its own sort of suicide this ridiculous world that destroys its finest products—and then, devoting one's mind entirely to supernatural things, sing a dirge over the ruins of all that here below seems beautiful and precious?

But then I pulled myself together. I told myself that human labor, whatever form it may take, must be essentially tenacious, patient, gentle. By uncomplainingly putting right the disorders and obstacles, a new order is taking shape and painfully clearing a place for itself in the world, an order by virtue of which the brutal shocks and blind disasters that still bruise and so often crush humanity as it blossoms within the chaotic complex of determinism will be reduced to a minimum. And I told myself that I would continue, should God spare me, to work at the earth's task.

~Silence~

Responsory

Life, as a whole, makes no mistakes.

Cosmic Canticle

We shall find again the essence and the splendor
of all the flowers, the lights,
we have had to surrender here and now
in order to be faithful to life.

Those beings whom here and now
we despair of ever reaching and influencing,
they too will be there,
united together at that central point in their being
which is at once the most vulnerable,
the most receptive and the most enriching.

There, even the least of our desires and our endeavors
will be gathered and preserved,
and be able to evoke instantaneous vibration
from the very heart of the universe.

~Intercessions~

Lord's Prayer

Lord of my childhood and Lord of my last days,
God, complete in Yourself
yet, for us, continually being born,
God, You offer Yourself to our worship as *evolver and evolving,*
the only being that can satisfy us.

Sweep away at last the clouds that still hide You,
the clouds of hostile prejudice and of false creeds.

You have become for my mind and heart
much more than God who was and who is:
You have become God who shall be.

CLOSING PRAYER

May the might of those invincible hands
direct and transfigure
for the great world You have in mind
that earthly travail which I have gathered into my heart
and now offer You in its entirety.
Remold it, rectify it, recast it
down to the depths from whence it springs.
You know how Your creatures can come into being only,
like shoot from stem,
as part of an endlessly renewed process of evolution.

Dark

The dead—they'll never wake from that dream.

INVOCATION

My God!
I prostrate myself before Your presence in the universe
now become living flame.

DOXOLOGY

God is eternal Being-in-itself
everywhere in process of formation for us.
God is the heart of everything.

OPENING VERSE

God can be grasped in and through every life.

But can God also be found in and through every death?
This is what perplexes us deeply.

Night Hymn

Make possible the flowering in the human heart
of this new universal love,
so often vainly dreamed of but now at last declaring itself
as both possible and necessary.

Notice this: if people on earth, all over the earth,
are ever to love one another
it is not enough for them to recognize in one another
the elements of a single something;
they must also, by developing a "planetary" consciousness,
become aware they are becoming a single *somebody*.

Antiphon

There is only one way into the greater life.

Night Psalm

The day will come when Earth, too,
bleached to a uniform whiteness, like a great fossil,
will be a mere gravitational cipher;
there will be no more movement on its surface,
and it will still hold all our bones.

What is descending upon us, therefore, from the sky
in the clearness of the nights,
is not a challenge to an insensate duel.
It is a supreme warning.

Down here, flesh—
elaborated by spirit in order to act and develop itself—
inevitably becomes, sooner or later,
a prison in which the soul suffocates;

and in consequence there is only one way
into the greater life open to natural organisms,
whether they belong to the individual or to Humankind
—and that way is Death.

ANTIPHON

Every star will know its own individual death.

NIGHT PSALM

Incessantly, like a trembling haze that vanishes,
a little spirit is released from the Earth
and evaporates around it:
the soul of those who have passed away.

By that same road must depart
the fully formed and matured Spirit of the great Monad.

Every star will know its own individual death:
in cold or conflagration, in intestine struggles
or in slumbering happiness.

The only true death, good death,
is obtained by a desperate effort on the part of the living
to be more pure, more stripped of everything,
more tense in their determination
to escape from the zone in which they are confined.

Happy the World that is to end in ecstasy!

Psalm Prayer

If I seal up the entry into my heart I must dwell in darkness.
But if my heart is open to You,
then at once through the pure intent of my will
the divine must flood into the universe.
Christ, flood into and over me, me and my cosmos.
How I long for this to be!

~Silence~

Litany

To know that we are not prisoners.
To know that there is a way out.

To know that there is air, and light, and love,
somewhere, beyond the reach of all death.

To know this, that it is neither an illusion nor a fairy story.

Closing Prayer

Teach us, Lord, how to contemplate the sphinx
without succumbing to its spell;
how to grasp the hidden mystery in the womb of death,
not by a refinement of human doctrine,
but in the simple concrete act
by which You plunged Yourself into matter
in order to redeem it.
Teach us to harness for You, the spiritual power of matter.

Saturday

Transforming Spirit

Dawn

*The time has come
when a new mysticism must emerge.*

INVOCATION

You come down, Lord, into this day which is now beginning!
Be present in small measure, in great measure,
more and more.

DOXOLOGY

To Terra Mater,
and through her to Christ Jesus,
above all things.

What is most vitally necessary to the thinking earth
is a faith—and a great faith—and ever more faith.

HYMN

Those who spread their sails in the right way
to the winds of the earth
will always find themselves borne by a current
towards the open seas.

The more nobly they will and act,
the more avid they become
for great and sublime aims to pursue.

Little by little the great breath of the universe
has insinuated itself into them
through the fissure of their humble but faithful action,
has broadened them, raised them up, borne them on.

It is God and God alone whom they pursue
through the reality of created things.
For them, interest lies truly *in* things,
in an absolute dependence upon God's presence in them.

The light of heaven
becomes perceptible and attainable to them
in the crystalline transparency of beings.

Within them and their most personal development,
it is not themselves that they are seeking,
but that which is greater than them,
to which they know that they are destined.

In their own view they no longer count, no longer exist;
they have forgotten and lost themselves
in the very endeavor which is making them perfect.
It is no longer the atom which lives,
but the universe within it.

Antiphon

Through the World, God penetrates us.

Psalm

Outside the group of our souls,
living Matter still contains
the countless Elements of spiritualization
scattered and diffused throughout the Universe:
energies for bodies,
stimulants for soul,
shades of beauty,
sparks of truth.

Through the World, God envelops us,
penetrates us, and creates us.

Like a little child still clinging to its mother's breast,
our spirit sends down all sorts of tendrils and roots
into Materia matrix.

It needs that material mother in order to live;
and the grand role of the soul is to extract—
to the last drop, were that possible—
the *spiritual power* generously stored
in the lower circles of the Universe.

It is the vocation, and the supreme joy, of every Human
to add to this spiritual Reserve
a truth, an impulse that works for good,
a new Element of whatever nature,
from which generations to come will draw nourishment
until the end of time.

ANTIPHON

In each soul, God loves the whole world.

PSALM

We must not forget that the human soul
is inseparable from the universe into which it is born.

In each soul, God loves and partly saves the whole world
which that soul sums up
in an incommunicable and particular way.

We, through our own activity,
must industriously assemble the widely scattered elements.

The labor of seaweed as it concentrates in its tissues
the substances scattered, in infinitesimal quantities,
throughout the vast layers of the ocean;

the industry of bees as they make honey
from the juices broadcast in so many flowers—

these are but pale images of the ceaseless working-over
that all the forces of the universe undergo in us
in order to reach the level of spirit.

PSALM PRAYER

No longer simply a religion of individuals and of heaven, but
a religion of humankind and of the earth—that is what we are
looking for at this moment, as the oxygen without which we
cannot breathe.

READING

We are now for the first time witnessing the inauguration of a
spiritual movement, intimately linked with the progress of the
tangible world regarded as one whole:

~ zest for unity in order to preserve the universal zest
for action;

~ a new faith conditioning a new humankind;
~ one single soul for the whole surface of the earth.

The world will never be converted to hopes of heaven, unless first converted to the hopes of the earth.

VERSICLE

The Universe yields,
it is plastic somehow, under the influence of faith;
it comes to life and grows warm.

~SILENCE~

RESPONSORY

A new vision of the universe calls for a new form of worship and a new method of action.

COSMIC CANTICLE

Eating, drinking, working, seeking;
creating truth or beauty or happiness—

all these things could have seemed to us disparate activities,
incapable of being reduced to terms of one another—
loving being no more than one of a number of branches
in this divergent psychical efflorescence.

Now that it is directed towards the Super-Christ,
the fascicle draws itself together.

Like the countless shades that combine in nature
to produce a single white light,
so the infinite modalities of action are fused,
without being confused,
in one single color under the mighty power
of the universal Christ.

And it is love that heads this movement:
love, not simply the common factor
through which the multiplicity of human activities
attains its cohesion,
but love, the higher, universal, and synthesized form
of spiritual energy,
in which all the other energies of the soul
are transformed and sublimated,
once they fall within the field of Omega.

In that center every activity is *amorized.*
A Super-humankind calls for a Super-Christ.
A Super-Christ calls for a *Super-Charity.*

~INTERCESSIONS~

LORD'S PRAYER

Lord of my childhood and Lord of my last days,
God, complete in Yourself

yet, for us, continually being born,
God, You offer Yourself to our worship as *evolver and evolving,*
the only being that can satisfy us.

Sweep away at last the clouds that still hide You,
the clouds of hostile prejudice and of false creeds.

You have become for my mind and heart
much more than God who was and who is:
You have become God who shall be.

Closing Prayer

You whose loving wisdom forms me
out of all the forces and all the hazards of the earth
grant that I may believe
and believe ardently and above all things
in Your active presence.

Day

*I can't help wondering how in these days
we should envisage a cathedral.*

Invocation

Lord—I make the whole earth my altar!
On it I offer You all the labors and sufferings of the world.

Doxology

To Terra Mater,
and through her to Christ Jesus,
above all things.

Exhortation

We must not allow timidity or modesty to turn us into poor artisans. If it is true that the development of the world can be influenced by our faith, then to let this power be dormant within us would indeed be unpardonable.

Antiphon

Add one stitch to the magnificent tapestry of life.

Psalm

Centration—
the only love which brings true happiness
is that which is expressed
in a spiritual progress effected in common.

Decentration—
like the first aviators and pioneers
we must re-polarize our lives
upon one greater than ourselves.

Do not be afraid that this means
that if we are to be happy
we must perform some remarkable feat
or do something quite out of the ordinary.

We have only to do what any one of us is capable of:
become conscious of our living solidarity
with one great Thing,
and then do the smallest thing in a great way.

We must add one stitch,
no matter how small it be,
to the magnificent tapestry of life.

We must discern the Immense which is building up
and whose magnetic pull is exerted at the very heart
of our own humblest activities and at their term.

We must discern it and cling to it—
when all is said and done,
that is the great secret of happiness.

It is in a deep and instinctive union
with the whole current of life
that the greatest of all joys is to be found.
—Super-centration.

Psalm Prayer

Some say, "Let us wait patiently until the Christ returns."
Others say, "Let us rather finish building the Earth."
Still others think, "To speed the Parousia,
let us complete the making of the Human on Earth."

MEDITATION

The God for whom our century is waiting must be:
- ~ as vast and mysterious as the Cosmos
- ~ as immediate and all-embracing as Life
- ~ as linked to our effort as Humankind

A God who made the World less mysterious or smaller,
or less important to us
than our heart and reason show it to be,
that God, less beautiful than the God we await—
will never more be the One to whom the Earth kneels.

PRAYER

All that really matters is devotion to something bigger than
ourselves. The more I devote myself in some way to the interests of the earth in its highest form, the more I belong to God.

~REFLECTION~

LESSON

The Arising of God: Contemporary humankind has passed
through a period of great illusion in imagining that, having
attained a better knowledge of themselves and the world, they
have no more need of religion. In reality, for anyone who can
see great conflict has merely strengthened the world's need
for belief. Having reached a higher stage in self-mastery, the

184

spirit of the earth is discovering a more and more vital need to worship from universal evolution. God emerges in our minds greater and more necessary than ever.

Collect

Let us put our trust in spiritual energies.
Let us take care not to reject the least ray of light
from any side.
Faith has need of all the truth.

Examen

Religion can become an opium. It is too often understood as a simple soothing of our woes. Its true function is to sustain and spur on the progress of life.

How can we fail to be struck by the revealing growth around us of a strong mystical current, actually nourished by the conviction that the universe, viewed in its complete workings, is ultimately lovable and loving?

Kyrie

Because, my God, I lack the soul-zeal
    and the integrity of Your saints. *Kyrie Eleison*
Because my God, I received from You
    an overwhelming sympathy for all that stirs
    within the dark mass of matter. *Christe Eleison*

Because, my God, I know myself to be
   irremediably less a child of heaven
   than a child of earth. *Kyrie Eleison*

BENEDICTION

In every context, try harder to lose yourself in God—so completely that you no longer even want to know whether you are doing much or little in this world—your sole happiness being the feeling that God is within you, at the beginning and the end of every desire and every act.

Dusk

*Await more steadfastly than ever
the coming of the Spirit of the Earth.*

INVOCATION

Lord, the luminosity and fragrance
which suffuse the universe
take on for me the lineaments of a body and a face: *You!*

DOXOLOGY

To Terra Mater,
and through her to Christ Jesus,
above all things.

OPENING VERSE

The power to appreciate and to open the heart
is indispensable to the awakening and the maintenance
of the mystical appetite.

EVENING HYMN

Let us establish ourselves in the *divine milieu.*
There we shall find ourselves
where the soul is most deep
and where matter is most dense.

There we shall discover,
where all its beauties flow together,
the ultra-vital, the ultra-sensitive,
the ultra-active point of the universe.

And, at the same time,
we shall feel the plenitude
of our powers of action and adoration
effortlessly ordered within our deepest selves.

ANTIPHON

No one can compel the gaze of God.

PSALM

A breeze passes in the night.
When did it spring up?
Whence does it come?
Whither is it going?

No one knows.
No one can compel the spirit,
the gaze or the light of God
to descend upon them.

On some given day
one suddenly becomes conscious
that they are alive to a particular perception of the divine
spread everywhere about them.

Question them.
When did this state begin for them?
They cannot tell.
All they know is that a new spirit has crossed their life:

"It began with a particular and unique resonance
which swelled each harmony,
with a diffused radiance which haloed each beauty.

All the elements of psychological life were in turn affected;
sensations, feelings, thoughts.
Day by day they became more fragrant,

more colored, more intense
by means of an indefinable thing—
the same thing.

Then the vague note, and fragrance, and light
began to define themselves.
And then, contrary to all expectation and all probability,
I began to feel what was ineffably common to all things.

The unity communicated itself to me
by giving me the gift of grasping it.
I had in fact acquired a new sense,
the sense of a new quality or of a new dimension.

Deeper still: a transformation had taken place for me
in the very perception of being.

Thenceforward being had become tangible and savorous;
and as it came to dominate all the forms which it assumed,
being itself began to draw me and to intoxicate me."

Antiphon

In the silence of the night, I can hear.

Psalm

Already, in the silence of the night,
I can hear through this world of tumult

a confused rustling as of crystalline needles
forming themselves into a pattern
or of birds huddling closer together in their nest—
a deep murmur of distress, of discomfort,
of well-being, of triumph,
rising up from the Unity which is reaching its fulfilment.

Psalm Prayer

Through every cleft
the world we perceive floods us with its riches—

food for the body, nourishment for the eyes,
harmony of sounds and fullness of the heart,
unknown phenomena and new truths—

all these treasures, all these stimuli, all these calls,
coming to us from the four corners of the world,
cross our consciousness at every moment.

Epistle

Seeing. We might say that the whole of life lies in that verb. Union increases only through an increase in consciousness, that is to say in vision. And that, doubtless, is why the history of the living world can be summarized as the elaboration of ever more perfect eyes within a cosmos in which there is always something more to be seen.

~Silence~

Responsory

Ahead of us there must lie something immortal.
To perceive it calls for training the inner eye.

Cosmic Canticle

Three things, tiny, fugitive:
a song, a sunbeam, a glance.

So, at first, I thought they had entered into me
in order to remain and be lost in me.

On the contrary:
they took possession of me, and bore me away.

Through the sharp tips of the three arrows
which had pierced me
the world itself had invaded my being
and had drawn me back into itself.

The vibration aroused a resonance in all my affections.
It drew me out of myself,
into a wider harmony than that which delights the senses,
into an ever richer and more spiritual rhythm
that was imperceptibly and endlessly
becoming the measure of all growth and all beauty.

I felt my body, my soul, and even my spirit
pass into the ethereal tint, unreal in its freshness,
that caressed my eyes.

Serene and iridescent,
its color bathed more than my senses;
it in some way impregnated my affections and thoughts.

I melted away in it,
lost in a strange yearning
to attain some individuality vaster and simpler than mine—
as though I had become pure light.

And, under the glance that fell upon me,
the shell in which my heart slumbered, burst open.

With pure and generous love,
a new energy penetrated into me—
or emerged from me, which, I cannot say—
that made me feel that I was as vast
and as loaded with richness as the universe.

~INTERCESSIONS~

LORD'S PRAYER

Lord of my childhood and Lord of my last days,
God, complete in Yourself
yet, for us, continually being born,

God, You offer Yourself to our worship as *evolver and evolving,*
the only being that can satisfy us.

Sweep away at last the clouds that still hide You,
the clouds of hostile prejudice and of false creeds.

You have become for my mind and heart
much more than God who was and who is:
You have become God who shall be.

Closing Prayer

Let there be revealed to us the possibility
of believing at the same time and wholly
in God and the World,
the one through the other.

Let this belief burst forth,
as it is ineluctably in process of doing
under the pressure of these seemingly opposed forces,
and then, we may be sure of it,
a great flame will illumine all things:

for a Faith will have been born (or reborn)
containing and embracing all others—
and, inevitably, it is the strongest Faith
which sooner or later must possess the Earth.

Dark

*We are all of us together carried
in the one world-womb.*

Invocation

Glittering gem of matter,
Pearl of the Cosmos!
Link with the incarnate personal Absolute,
Queen and Mother of all things.

Doxology

To Terra Mater,
and through her to Christ Jesus,
above all things.

Opening Verse

The great animating Power, to which it is so good to entrust ourselves, seems—in a motherly way—to have brought the inner and outer forces of the world into harmony around me.

Night Hymn

I would like to speak
what I hear murmuring in me
like a voice or a song which are not of me,
but of the World in me.

I would like to express the thoughts of someone
who, having finally penetrated the partitions and ceilings
of little countries, little coteries, little sects,
rises above all these categories
and finds themself a child and citizen of the Earth.

There is first of all the deep joy,
which we owe to our new perspectives on Life,
of feeling our being expand to the measure
of all the past, all the future, all space:
our rootedness in Matter
which wraps us round, weaves us, binds us together,
and is spiritualized in us.

It is the Note of the All, joyous and magnificent.

Antiphon

The night of everything is within us.

Night Psalm

We know ourselves and set our own course
but within an incredibly small radius of light.

Immediately beyond
lies impenetrable darkness,
though it is full of presences—
the night of everything that is within us
and around us, without us and in spite of us.

In this darkness,
as vast, rich, troubled and complex
as the past and the present of the universe,
we are not inert;
we react, because we undergo.

But this reaction,
which operates without our control
by an unknown prolongation of our being,
is still a part of our passivity.

In fact, everything beyond a certain distance is dark,
and yet everything is full of being around us.

This is the darkness,
heavy with promises and threats,
which we will have to illuminate and animate
with the divine presence.

Antiphon

I found the current I dare to call my life.

Night Psalm

I took the lamp and leaving the zone
of everyday occupations and relationships
where everything seems clear,
I went down into my inmost self,
to the deep abyss
whence I feel dimly that my power of action emanates.

But as I moved further and further away
from the conventional certainties
by which social life is superficially illuminated,
I became aware that I was losing contact with myself.

At each step of the descent
a new person was disclosed within me
of whose name I was no longer sure,
and who no longer obeyed me.

And when I had to stop my exploration
because the path faded from beneath my steps,

I found a bottomless abyss at my feet,
and out of it came—
arising I know not from where—
the current which I dare to call my life.

Stirred by my discovery,
I then wanted to return to the light of day
and forget the disturbing enigma
in the comfortable surroundings of familiar things—
to begin living again at the surface
without imprudently plumbing the depths of the abyss.

But then, beneath this very spectacle of the turmoil of life,
there reappeared, before my newly-opened eyes,
the unknown that I wanted to escape.

This time it was not hiding at the bottom of an abyss;
it disguised its presence in the innumerable strands
which form the web of chance,
the very stuff of which the universe
and my own small individuality are woven.

After the consciousness of being something other
and something greater than myself—
a second thing made me dizzy:

namely, the supreme improbability,
the tremendous unlikelihood
of finding myself existing in the heart of a world
that has survived and succeeded in being a world.

Psalm Prayer

To Your deep inspiration which commands me to be,
I shall respond by taking great care
never to stifle nor distort nor waste
my power to love and to do.

To Your all-embracing providence
which shows the next step to take and the next rung to climb,
I shall respond by my care
never to miss an opportunity of rising,
towards the level of spirit.

~Silence~

Litany

Every exhalation that passes through me,
envelops me or captivates me,
emanates from the heart of God;
like a subtle and essential energy,
it transmits the pulsations of God's will.

Every encounter that brings me a caress,
that spurs me on, that comes as a shock to me,
that bruises or breaks me,
is a contact with the hand of God,
which assumes countless forms
and yet always commands our worship.

Every element of which I am made up
is an overflow from God.

When I surrender myself to the embrace
of the visible and tangible universe,
I am able to be in communion
with the invisible that purifies,
and to incorporate myself in the Spirit without blemish.

Closing Prayer

The earth mother can indeed take me now
into the immensity of her arms.
She can enlarge me with her life,
or take me back into her primordial dust.
She can adorn herself for me
with every allurement, every horror, every mystery.
She can intoxicate me
with the scent of her tangibility and her unity.
She can throw me to my knees in expectancy
of what is maturing in her womb.

But all her enchantments can no longer harm me,
since she has become for me,
more than herself and beyond herself,
the body of the One who is and who is to come.

Tomorrow

Toward Omega

Dawn

I am a pilgrim of the future.

INVOCATION

The sun is rising ahead.
God, advance to meet us!

DOXOLOGY

Sense of the human;
sense of the earth;
sense of an Omega:
three progressive stages of one and the same illumination.

OPENING VERSE

I am a pilgrim of the future on my way back from a journey
made entirely in the past.

Hymn

The rays in whose light we bask
do not diverge from the past,
but converge towards the future.

The sun is rising ahead.

These luminous shades
that we see floating over the world's beginnings
are therefore reflections from ahead.

Antiphon

The only thing worth the trouble of finding
has never yet existed.

Psalm

Cosmically speaking, humanity is still quite young.
What are a few tens or even a few hundreds of millennia
if we wish to study the curve of thought
in its shortest harmonics?

We could not plunge far in this direction
without touching bottom.
Then at last we will have understood
the essential word whispered to us
by the ruins, the fossils and the ashes:

the only thing worth the trouble of finding
is what has never yet existed.

The only task worthy of our efforts
is to construct the future.

ANTIPHON

A center lies ahead.

PSALM

What gives the universe around us its consistence
is not the apparent solidity of the ephemeral materials
from which bodies are made.

Rather it is the flame of organic development
which has been running through the world
since the beginning of time,
constantly building itself up.

With all its weight behind it,
the world is being impelled upon a center
which lies ahead of it.

Far from being impermanent and accidental,
it is souls, and alliances of souls,
it is the energies of souls,

that alone progress infallibly,
and it is they alone that will endure.

Psalm Prayer

The world does not hold together *from below* but *from above*.
When everything else, after concentrating or being dissipated,
has passed away, spirit will remain.

Reading

Savor that rich delight of being a "citizen of the Earth." Yes, I
believe we are approaching the moment when new affinities—
the true panhuman affinities—will break down nationalistic
boundaries, in politics as in religion. And I imagine that, in
accordance with a general law of matter, this enormous quan-
titative modification will produce new qualities on our Earth.

I have an impression that the earth, while retaining its
prodigious power of communicating the Divine to us through
all its being, is becoming paler and paler to me as regards its
present and its past.

It is the future that is fascinating, and I see it all ablaze with
God springing up everywhere.

Versicle

We shall never know all that the Incarnation still expects of the
world's potentialities. We shall never put enough hope in the
growing unity of humankind.

RESPONSORY

At the heart of our universe, each soul exists for God.

COSMIC CANTICLE

The universal-Christ assumes the place
and fulfils the function of Omega Point:
we shall then find that a warm light
spreads from top to bottom
and over the whole cross-section of the cosmic layers,
rising up from the nethermost depths of things.

With cosmogenesis being transformed to *Christogenesis,*
it is the stuff, the main stream,
the very being of the world
which is now being personalized.

Someone, and no longer something,
is in gestation in the universe.

To believe and to serve was not enough:
we now find
that it is becoming not only possible but imperative
literally to love evolution.

LORD'S PRAYER

Lord of my childhood and Lord of my last days,
God, complete in Yourself
yet, for us, continually being born,
God, You offer Yourself to our worship as *evolver and evolving,*
the only being that can satisfy us.

Sweep away at last the clouds that still hide You,
the clouds of hostile prejudice and of false creeds.

You have become for my mind and heart
much more than God who was and who is:
You have become God who shall be.

CLOSING PRAYER

The greatest event in the history of the Earth, now taking place,
may indeed be the gradual discovery, by those with eyes to see,
not merely of Some Thing but of Some One at the peak created
by the convergence of the evolving Universe upon itself.

Day

May Christ-Omega keep me always young.

INVOCATION

Prime Mover and Ultimate Gatherer ahead:
God, spring up everywhere!

DOXOLOGY

Sense of the human;
sense of the earth;
sense of an Omega:
three progressive stages of one and the same illumination.

211

Exhortation

The time is close at hand when humankind will see that in virtue of its position in a cosmic evolution which it has become capable of discovering and criticizing, it now stands biologically between the alternatives of suicide and worship.

Antiphon

Withdraw into God in the heart of the mystic night.

Psalm

Finally, everything will be ineffably transformed
on the other side.
It is not inconceivable that a phase of this metamorphosis
should take place here on earth.
The day may come when the surface of the earth
is under total cultivation or has become uninhabitable,
and humanity's sole concern will be to withdraw
more directly and deeply into God
in the heart of the mystic night.

I do not see that the moment has yet come.
Laborers are still needed to sustain those at their orisons—
and one must be able to explain to them
that they are working in Christ,
even in tilling the soil.

Psalm Prayer

The earth around us is psychically raised to a white-hot temperature. Never, since its globe appeared in space, has it vibrated with more spiritual intensity. What we are suffering from is not a drop in internal energy but its mounting pressure.

Meditation

The whole future of the Earth, as of religion, depends on the awakening of our faith in the future as though awakening from a dream. We are beginning to realize that our nobility consists in serving, like intelligent atoms, the work proceeding in the Universe.

We have discovered that there is a Whole, of which we are the elements. We have found the world in our own souls.

~Reflection~

Prayer

To share in a hallowed unity, even for a split second, is enough to enable us to glimpse the future promised to our species, and to find the road that will lead us to it.

Lesson

Humanity, for each of us, is not only that stem which supports, unifies, preserves. It is the leading shoot which contains the achievements of the future. We must believe in humanity more than in ourselves, or else we will lose hope. Thus, on the level of the human (or of the noosphere) the progressive advance of earthly life does not fragment. Unities of a new kind are formed, to act as more perfect constituents and intended for a superior organization. The general convergence which constitutes universal evolution is not completed by hominization. There are not only minds on the earth. The world continues and there will be a spirit of the earth.

Collect

All around us, the thinking envelope of the Earth—the Noosphere—is adding to its internal fibers and tightening its network; and at the same time its internal temperature is rising, and with this its psychic potential. With every day that passes it becomes a little more impossible for us to act or think otherwise than collectively. The Noosphere, in short, is a stupendous thinking machine.

Examen

Isn't the past, viewed from a certain angle, transformable into future? Isn't a wider awareness of what is and what has been the essential basis of all spiritual progress? Isn't my whole life sustained by the single hope of co-operating in a forward march?

Since we have learned to see the universe not as a thing but as a process, the age-old and exasperating question of "the human's *place* in nature" has become that of "the human's *movement* in nature."

214

In other words, the problem is not so much to know what the human is, or even how the human, historically, appeared on earth, but rather to decide whether, in the framework of time, there is or is not, for us, something ultra-human, lying ahead of us.

KYRIE

Flung into existence, we are forced to advance into a future
    which terrifies us. *Kyrie Eleison*
The more we believe in life, the more the Universe
    is able to build itself around us. *Christe Eleison*
The bolder we are, the more the Universe
    is able to build its mystical reality. *Kyrie Eleison*

BENEDICTION

Above all, through our Lord's kindness and great love,
may we be so united in our Lord
that God may be seen in all that we do.
That is what I ask for you, and for myself, and for all I love.

Dusk

*Love, like thought, is still in full growth
in the noosphere.*

INVOCATION

God, prime psychic mover ahead:
spring up everywhere!

DOXOLOGY

Sense of the human;
sense of the earth;
sense of an Omega:
three progressive stages of one and the same illumination.

Opening Verse

Of all the living things we know,
none is more really, more intensely living than the noosphere.

Evening Hymn

God, the personal and loving Infinite,
is the Source, the motive Force,
and the End of the Universe.

The world emerged from the heart of God's creative power,
laden with rich seed.
The world came from God,
to return enriched and purified to God.
Such is the design of the universe.

To open wide our hearts
to the love of the Being
who animates every creature
as they are drawn in;

to shut out from our affections
the transient passions of here below;

to die that we may rise again—
there we have the secret of life,
simple and yet difficult,
that our good will has to decipher.

Antiphon

A common venture, a common destiny.

Psalm

Until now, people were living both dispersed
and at the same time closed in on themselves,
like passengers in a ship
who have met by chance below decks
with no idea of its mobile character and its motion.

They could think of nothing to do on the earth
that brought them together
but to quarrel or amuse themselves.

And now, by chance,
or rather as a normal effect of growing older,
we have just opened our eyes.

The boldest of us have found their way to the deck.
They have seen the vessel that was carrying us along.
They have marked the creaming of her bow wave.
They have realized that there are boilers to be stoked
and a wheel to be manned.

And most important of all,
they have seen the clouds floating overhead,

they have savored the sweet scent of the Western Isles,
over the curve of the horizon:

it ceases to be the restless human to-and-fro,
it is no longer a drifting—
it is the voyage.

Another humankind
must inevitably emerge from this vision,
one of which we have as yet no idea,
but one which I can already feel stirring
through the old humankind,
whenever the chances of life
bring me into contact with another.

However alien they may be to me
by nationality, class, race or religion,
I find them closer to me than a sibling,
because they, too, have seen the ship
and they, too, feel that we are steaming ahead.
The sense of a common venture,
and in consequence of a common destiny.

ANTIPHON

First, *be.* Second, *love.* Finally, *worship.*

PSALM

As the transformation follows its natural line of progress
we can foresee the time
when humanity will understand what it is,
animated by one single heart,
to be united together in wanting, hoping for,
and loving the same things at the same time.

The humankind of tomorrow
is emerging from the mists of the future,
and we can actually see it taking shape:
a superhumankind,
much more conscious, much more powerful,
and much more unanimous than our own.

And at the same time
we can detect an underlying but deeply rooted feeling
that if we are to reach the ultimate of our own selves,
we must do more than link our own being
with a handful of other beings
selected from the thousands that surround us:
we must form one whole with all simultaneously.

We must, then, do more than develop our own selves,
more than give ourselves to another who is our equal.
We must surrender and attach our lives
to one who is greater than ourselves.

In other words: first, *be.* Second, *love.* Finally, *worship.*

Psalm Prayer

The day will come when, after harnessing the ether, the winds, the tides, and gravitation, we shall harness for God the energies of love. And, on that day, for the second time in the history of the world, we will have discovered fire.

Epistle

Have the gospels anything to say about the modern industrial crisis; and is there anything in them that points to reversal? My hope is that, from awakening to the threat of a mechanized Earth, we shall be forced into the conception of and the belief in a spiritual structure of the world.

This is the very moment, paradoxically, for humanity to discover the biological value, and the possible extension, of the only energy which can group and achieve individuals, without turning them into a gadget or a slave: a mutual form of love, based on the consciousness of a common Something (or rather Somebody) into which all together we converge.

The awakening of the sense of the human is a contemporary phenomenon, which has brought into the world something completely new. The awakening of the sense of the human cannot be anything but the dawn of a new epiphany.

~Silence~

Responsory

Only a God who is functionally and totally *Omega*
can satisfy us.
Where shall we find such a God?
Who at last will give evolution its own God?

Cosmic Canticle

There, above all,
we can count upon creative energy awaiting us,
ready to transform us in a way
that goes beyond anything
that the human eye has seen or human ear has heard.

Who can say what God might make of us,
if we dared, relying on the Word,
to follow God's precepts to the uttermost,
and surrender ourselves to God's providence?

For love of our Creator and of the universe,
we must fling ourselves boldly
into the crucible of the world to come.

~Intercessions~

Lord's Prayer

Lord of my childhood and Lord of my last days,
God, complete in Yourself
yet, for us, continually being born,
God, You offer Yourself to our worship as *evolver and evolving,*
the only being that can satisfy us.

Sweep away at last the clouds that still hide You,
the clouds of hostile prejudice and of false creeds.

You have become for my mind and heart
much more than God who was and who is:
You have become God who shall be.

Closing Prayer

Lord God, for my (very lowly) part,
I would wish to be the apostle
—the evangelist—
of Your Christ in the universe.
For You gave me the gift of sensing,
beneath the incoherence of the surface,
the deep, living unity.

Dark

Futurism, Universalism, Personalism:
three pillars on which
the future rests.

INVOCATION

Primacy of the Future.
God—spring up everywhere!

DOXOLOGY

Sense of the human;
sense of the earth;
sense of an Omega:
three progressive stages of one and the same illumination.

Opening Verse

Omega, in which all things converge,
from which all things radiate.

Night Hymn

The mystical Christ has not yet attained full growth;
and therefore, the same is true of the cosmic Christ.

Both of these are simultaneously
in the state of being and of becoming;
and it is from the prolongation
of this process of becoming
that all created activity ultimately springs.

Christ is the end point of the evolution,
even the natural evolution, of all beings;
and therefore, evolution is holy.

Antiphon

Humanity is not the center of the universe,
but the arrow pointing the way.

Night Psalm

Humankind is not the center of the universe
as once we thought in our simplicity,

but something much more wonderful—
the arrow pointing the way
to the final unification of the world in terms of life.

The human alone constitutes the last-born,
the freshest, the most complicated,
the most subtle of all the successive layers of life.

What evolution perceives of itself in humanity
by reflecting itself in them
is enough to dispel or at least to correct
these paradoxical appearances.

Certainly, in our innermost being
we all feel the weight,
the stock of obscure powers, good or bad,
a sort of definite and unalterable *quantum*
handed down to us once and for all from the past.

ANTIPHON

This new star, the earth of tomorrow.

NIGHT PSALM

God is no longer seen
as standing immediately above humanity:
there is an intermediate magnitude,
with its accompanying train of promises and duties.

Thus, without leaving the world,
humans are now discovering above themselves
some sort of object of worship,
something greater than themselves:

and it is the appearance of the earth of tomorrow—
of this new star,
channeling into itself
the religious forces of the world.

Psalm Prayer

May God preserve within me the deep taste, and the sort of lucid ecstasy, that intoxicate me with the joy of Being—a joy drunk in as though from an everlasting spring.

When I'm immersed in rocks and fossils, I sometimes feel an indefinable bliss when I remember that I possess—in a total, incorruptible, and living Element—the supreme Principle in which all subsists and comes to life.

What science or philosophy is comparable to the knowledge of that Reality? May God give that gift to you and me and preserve it within us. With the possession of that light and that fire one can go everywhere, enlightening oneself and nourishing oneself on everything.

~Silence~

LITANY

Lord, You offered my aspirations and my efforts
the inner shelter of the divine Essence,
mysteriously incorporated in our universe,
and You said to me:

"*I am at hand.*
I am at hand,
at the common heart of your own being and of all things,
I am at hand
to welcome even the wildest of your longings and
I am at hand
to assure you that not one single fragment
of what is useful in them will be lost to God.
I am at hand
ready to save for those who are to come
the treasure that would otherwise be lost today,
but which the future will inherit.

"One day I shall pass on to another, whose name I know,
the thought that is in your mind.

"And when that one speaks and is heard,
it is your voice that will be listened to.

"It is I who am the true bond that holds the World together.
Without me, even though beings may seem to make contact

with one another, they are divided by an abyss.
In me, they meet, in spite of the chaos of time and space.

"I am at hand to fructify and ease your labors.
But above all, I am at hand
to take over your work and consummate it."

Closing Prayer

Lord Jesus,
You are the center toward which all things are moving: if it be possible, make a place for us all in the company of those elect and holy ones whom Your loving care has liberated one by one from the chaos of our present existence and who now are being slowly incorporated into You in the unity of the new earth.

Postscript

My very dear friend. I pray for you daily when I ask God's protection for those who are nearest to me "in heart, in thought, and in science"—and you are included in all three categories. Pierre (LT, 104)

Afterword

A Brief Note on Composition

Libby Osgood

To compose this book, Kathleen and I put Teilhard's notion of the *noosphere*—the interconnected thinking layer of Earth—to the test as we relied on Zoom for our intergenerational and cross-discipline conversations, never meeting in person, but only virtually. We scoured over 5,600 pages of Teilhard's letters and essays, extracting passages that drew us into contemplative prayer. Whispers of "wow" and sometimes "ow" echoed during our selection process, as the power of Teilhard's vision resonated across the internet. We faithfully preserved as much of Teilhard's original language and structure as possible, making only minor modifications to ensure the text was inclusive, clearly communicated, and retained the original intent.

First, recognizing that since Teilhard's moment, religious and social language have evolved beyond binary terms, we adapted

233

gendered terms with more inclusive language. Male pronouns for "God" and "Christ" were replaced with the proper nouns for each, except in a few instances where the substitution would be distracting. The gendered terms "brothers and sisters" became "kin," and the pronouns "he, him, his" became the singular implementation of "they, them, theirs."

Second, whereas English translations of Teilhard's work use the word "man" when referring to the collective sense of humankind, Teilhard uses the French term "humain." For example, the French title for *Le Phénomène Humain* was originally translated to English as *The Phenomenon of Man*, but in a more recent edition it is translated as *The Human Phenomenon*. Following this understanding, in most instances, we used the more inclusive terms "human" or "humanity" in place of "man."

Lastly, we worked to present Teilhard's writing style as clearly as possible. He often wrote in a conversational mode with parenthetical thoughts inserted throughout his sentences. In order to clarify his message and preserve a prayerful spirit, we edited some explanatory phrases, and elected not to use ellipses as these would also detract from the contemplative flow of his thought.

In our *Book of Hours*, as we pray throughout the week, we proceed evolutively through Teilhard's themes. Beginning with the birth of the universe and the growing presence of Christ in the cosmos, we move to the emergence of the Earth, humanity, and consciousness, and then onto work, suffering, and visionary faith. The last day looks to the future, "Tomorrow: Toward Omega," as Teilhard sees us being drawn in *from* the future.

Each "hour" (Dawn, Day, Dusk, and Dark) evokes a specific mood to support us as we transition through our days on Earth. For example, the Dawn hour welcomes the day, and the prayers are an invitation to greater wakefulness and praise. The Day hour is focused on work, challenging us with exhortations and examens, propelling us on throughout our tasks. The Dusk hour is a chance to reflect on the lived day, offering gratitude and peaceful transition into the evening. Lastly, the Dark hour is meditative, to lull us into the close of the day and feed our dreams.

Similarly, each of the prayers has a specific intention. The first line of each hour offers a "breath prayer" intended to linger in our thoughts like a mantra, until the next hour begins. The invocations, verses, and antiphons call us to prayer. The hymns are Teilhard's more lyrical pieces reminiscent of song, while the psalms open us to a spiritual conversation. The canticles express praise while the litanies provide rhythmic insight. The exhortations challenge us to right action while the examens invite us to right mindfulness. The meditations inspire us while the *kyries* beg for intercession and mercy, and the doxologies are moments of praise repeated throughout each day connecting the hours together. The Teilhardian *Lord's Prayer* repeated daily at Dawn and Dusk was excavated from a single excerpt of Teilhard's writings and echoes the prayer that Jesus taught us.

As Teilhard once penned, "Thus we have reached the end of our inquiry" (SC, 137). So too, our passion project to create a Book of Hours using Teilhard's own words has come to an end. We pray that Teilhard may become for us an inspiring and transformational spiritual master, to intensify our love of the Earth as we find God in each tiny atom and in the multitude of enormous galaxies. May Teilhard's dedication to "those who love the world" (DM, 11) help each one of us to sense and express the "Hymn of the Universe" that is resonating in each one of us.

Abbreviations

References

Sunday Dawn
Breath Prayer p. 77 in HU
Invocation p. 129 in WTW
Doxology p. 212 in WTW
Opening Verse p. 84 in HE
Hymn pp. 15–16 in HM
Antiphon & Psalm pp. 46–47 in DM
Antiphon & Psalm pp. 132, 134 in DM
Psalm Prayer p. 112 in DM
Reading pp. 271–273 in AE
Versicle p. 14 in HU
Responsory p. 81 in WTW
Cosmic Canticle p. 28 in HU
Lord's Prayer pp. 56, 58 in HM
Closing Prayer p. 215 in WTW

Sunday Day
Breath Prayer p. 171 in AM
Invocation p. 129 in WTW
Doxology p. 212 in WTW

Exhortation p. 180 in SC
Antiphon & Psalm p. 112 in DM
Psalm Prayer pp. 83–84 in HE
Meditation pp. 78–79 in DM
Prayer p. 31 in HU
Lesson p. 48 in WTW
Collect p. 203 in HM
Examen p. 107 in WTW
Kyrie p. 58 in HE
Benediction p. 83 in LTF

Sunday Dusk

Breath Prayer p. 27 in WTW
Invocation p. 129 in WTW
Doxology p. 212 in WTW
Opening Verse p. 27 in WTW
Evening Hymn p. 14 in HU
Antiphon & Psalm pp. 119–120 in DM
Antiphon & Psalm pp. 121, 123, 124 in WTW
Psalm Prayer p. 27 in WTW
Epistle pp. 32–33 in LTF
Responsory p. 121 in DM
Cosmic Canticle p. 47 in DM
Lord's Prayer pp. 56, 58 in HM
Closing Prayer p. 32 in LTF

Sunday Dark

Breath Prayer p. 45 in DM
Invocation pp. 129–130 in WTW

Doxology p. 212 in WTW
Opening Verse p. 27 in WTW
Night Hymn p. 132 note in CE
Antiphon & Night Psalm pp. 58–59 in DM
Antiphon & Night Psalm pp. 58–59 in DM
Psalm Prayer p. 48 in WTW
Litany pp. 51–52 in WTW
Closing Prayer p. 48 in WTW

Monday Dawn

Breath Prayer p. 77 in SC
Invocation p. 14 in FM
Doxology p. 61 in WTW
Opening Verse p. 31 in HU
Hymn p. 128 in DM
Antiphon & Psalm p. 62 in SC
Antiphon & Psalm pp. 59–60 in SC
Psalm Prayer p. 29 in CE
Reading p. 103 in SC
Versicle p. 159 in HU
Responsory p. 88 in HU
Cosmic Canticle pp. 20–21 in HU
Lord's Prayer pp. 56, 58 in HM
Closing Prayer pp. 110–111 in WTW

Monday Day

Breath Prayer p. 213 in WTW
Invocation p. 178 in MM
Doxology p. 61 in WTW

Exhortation pp. 114–115 in HU
Antiphon & Psalm pp. 33–35 in SC
Psalm Prayer p. 110 in SC
Meditation p. 79 in SC
Prayer p. 163 in CE
Lesson pp. 15–16 in SC
Collect p. 91 in HE
Examen p. 76 in DM
Kyrie p. 125 in SC
Benediction p. 216 in WTW

MONDAY DUSK

Breath Prayer p. 117 in HM
Invocation p. 58 in HM
Doxology p. 61 in WTW
Opening Verse p. 216 in WTW
Evening Hymn p. 298 in WTW
Antiphon & Psalm pp. 60–61 in SC
Antiphon & Psalm p. 30 in HU
Psalm Prayer pp. 74–76 in SC
Epistle p. 48 in LTF
Responsory p. 49 in HU
Cosmic Canticle p. 97 in PM and p. 150 in HU
Lord's Prayer pp. 56, 58 in HM
Closing Prayer p. 298 in WTW

MONDAY DARK

Breath Prayer p. 7 in LLS
Invocation p. 216 in WTW

Doxology p. 61 in WTW
Opening Verse p. 75 in CE
Night Hymn p. 208 in WTW
Antiphon & Night Psalm p. 146 in WTW
Antiphon & Night Psalm p. 16 in HU
Psalm Prayer p. 75 in CE
Litany p. 146 in DM
Closing Prayer pp. 55–56 in HM

TUESDAY DAWN

Breath Prayer p. 20 in HU
Invocation p. 57 in LTF
Doxology pp. 66–67 in HU
Opening Verse p. 14 in WTW
Hymn p. 15 in HU
Antiphon & Psalm p. 12 in HU
Antiphon & Psalm pp. 26, 42 in VP
Psalm Prayer p. 185 in CE
Reading pp. 67–68 in PM
Versicle p. 47 in HE
Responsory p. 127 in HU
Cosmic Canticle pp. 65–66 in HU
Lord's Prayer pp. 56, 58 in HM
Closing Prayer p. 127 in DM

TUESDAY DAY

Breath Prayer p. 141 in HE
Invocation p. 123 in LT
Doxology pp. 66–67 in HU

Exhortation pp. 127, 36 in LTF
Antiphon & Psalm pp. 107–108 in HM
Psalm Prayer p. 18 in HU and p. 35 in HM
Meditation p. 32 in WTW
Prayer p. 73 in HU
Lesson p. 130 in WTW
Collect p. 115 in DM
Examen p. 38 in HE
Kyrie pp. 19–20, 47 in AE
Benediction p. 61 in MM

TUESDAY DUSK

Breath Prayer p. 132 in HU
Invocation p. 191 in HM
Doxology pp. 66–67 in HU
Opening Verse pp. 264–265 in PM
Evening Hymn p. 140 in DM
Antiphon & Psalm pp. 75–77 in LTF
Antiphon & Psalm pp. 46–47 in TF
Psalm Prayer p. 207 in WTW
Epistle p. 182 in WTW
Responsory p. 204 in TF
Cosmic Canticle pp. 66–67 in HU
Lord's Prayer pp. 56, 58 in HM
Closing Prayer p. 216 in WTW

TUESDAY DARK

Breath Prayer p. 15 in HM
Invocation p. 17 in HM

Doxology pp. 66–67 in HU
Opening Verse p. 122 in LTF
Night Hymn p. 28 in WTW
Antiphon & Night Psalm pp. 238, 245 in VP
Antiphon & Night Psalm p. 124 in LT
Psalm Prayer p. 31 in WTW
Litany pp. 73–74 in HU
Closing Prayer p. 74 in HU

Wednesday Dawn

Breath Prayer p. 124 in HE
Invocation p. 15 in HU
Doxology pp. 75, 90 in CE
Opening Verse p. 58 in LTF
Hymn pp. 125–126 in WTW
Antiphon & Psalm pp. 137, 153, 160 in PM
Antiphon & Psalm p. 24 in SC
Psalm Prayer p. 126 in WTW
Reading pp. 23–24 in HE
Versicle p. 102 in LTF
Responsory p. 202 in TF
Cosmic Canticle pp. 150, 153 in HE
Lord's Prayer pp. 56, 58 in HM
Closing Prayer p. 128 in WTW

Wednesday Day

Breath Prayer p. 70 in DM
Invocation p. 15 in HU
Doxology pp. 75, 90 in CE

Exhortation p. 62 in WTW
Antiphon & Psalm p. 199 in HM
Psalm Prayer pp. 58–59 in LTF
Meditation p. 165 in PM
Prayer p. 26 in HU
Lesson pp. 96–97 in HE
Collect p. 15 in WTW
Examen pp. 227, 230 in PM
Kyrie p. 138 in HM
Benediction p. 145 in DM

WEDNESDAY DUSK
Breath Prayer p. 108 in CE
Invocation p. 15 in HU
Doxology pp. 75, 90 in CE
Opening Verse p. 92 in AM
Evening Hymn p. 60 in CE
Antiphon & Psalm pp. 38, 40 in AE
Antiphon & Psalm p. 38 in CE
Psalm Prayer p. 187 in HM
Epistle p. 57 in MM
Responsory p. 49 in DM
Cosmic Canticle pp. 84, 88 in FM
Lord's Prayer pp. 56, 58 in HM
Closing Prayer p. 139 in HU

WEDNESDAY DARK
Breath Prayer p. 232 in PM
Invocation p. 15 in HU

Doxology pp. 75, 90 in CE

Opening Verse p. 186 in HM

Night Hymn pp. 32–33 in HE

Antiphon & Night Psalm pp. 183, 185 in HM

Antiphon & Night Psalm p. 41 in LTF

Psalm Prayer p. 26 in HU

Litany pp. 24, 18 in VP, p. 78 in MPN, and pp. 114, 121, 138 in AM

Closing Prayer p. 79 in DM

Thursday Dawn

Breath Prayer p. 58 in HU

Invocation pp. 27–28 in HU

Doxology p. 61 in HU

Opening Verse pp. 56–57 in HU

Hymn p. 64 in DM

Antiphon & Psalm pp. 48–49 in HE

Antiphon & Psalm p. 12 in HU

Psalm Prayer p. 94 in LTF

Reading p. 21 in TF

Versicle p. 125 in TF and p. 25 in VP

Responsory p. 121 in HU

Cosmic Canticle p. 13 in HU

Lord's Prayer pp. 56, 58 in HM

Closing Prayer p. 24 in HU

Thursday Day

Breath Prayer p. 169 in WTW

Invocation p. 128 in WTW

Doxology p. 61 in HU
Exhortation p. 61 in HU
Antiphon & Psalm p. 139 in DM
Psalm Prayer p. 111 in FM
Meditation pp. 101–102 in SC
Prayer p. 128 in WTW
Lesson p. 24 in HE
Collect p. 46 in FM
Examen pp. 133–134 in FM
Kyrie p. 128 in SC and p. 134 in FM
Benediction pp. 61–62 in HU

Thursday Dusk

Breath Prayer p. 220 in MM
Invocation p. 120 in WTW
Doxology p. 61 in HU
Opening Verse pp. 56–57 in HU
Evening Hymn pp. 139–140 in HM
Antiphon & Psalm p. 148 in HU
Antiphon & Psalm pp. 55–56 in DM
Psalm Prayer p. 56 in DM
Epistle pp. 79–80 in MM
Responsory p. 214 in HM
Cosmic Canticle p. 61 in WTW
Lord's Prayer pp. 56, 58 in HM
Closing Prayer p. 220 in MM

Thursday Dark

Breath Prayer p. 138 in DM
Invocation p. 120 in WTW

Doxology p. 61 in HU
Opening Verse p. 60 in HU
Night Hymn p. 139 in HU
Antiphon & Night Psalm pp. 137–138 in DM
Antiphon & Night Psalm p. 12 in HU
Psalm Prayer p. 120 in WTW
Litany p. 66 in DM
Closing Prayer p. 80 in DM

Friday Dawn

Breath Prayer p. 247 in WTW
Invocation p. 42 in DM
Doxology p. 50 in HU
Opening Verse p. 84 in DM
Hymn pp. 93–94 in HU and p. 65 in WTW
Antiphon & Psalm p. 86 in DM
Antiphon & Psalm pp. 126–127 in WTW
Psalm Prayer pp. 25–26 in HU
Reading pp. 247–248 in AE
Versicle p. 107 in LTF
Responsory p. 107 in LTF
Cosmic Canticle p. 113 in DM
Lord's Prayer pp. 56, 58 in HM
Closing Prayer p. 22 in HU

Friday Day

Breath Prayer p. 50 in HE
Invocation pp. 22–23 in HU
Doxology p. 50 in HU
Exhortation p. 126 in MM

Antiphon & Psalm p. 131 in WTW
Psalm Prayer p. 143 in WTW and p. 132 in VP
Meditation p. 137 in DM
Prayer p. 61 in WTW
Lesson p. 68 in WTW
Collect p. 137 in DM
Examen p. 137 in DM
Kyrie p. 137 in DM
Benediction p. 8 in LLS

Friday Dusk

Breath Prayer p. 105 in WTW
Invocation p. 42 in DM
Doxology p. 50 in HU
Opening Verse pp. 250–251 in LLS
Evening Hymn p. 68 in HU
Antiphon & Psalm p. 120 in HU
Antiphon & Psalm p. 104 in LTF
Psalm Prayer p. 55 in HM
Epistle p. 123 in MM
Responsory p. 213 in HM
Cosmic Canticle pp. 144–145 in HU
Lord's Prayer pp. 56, 58 in HM
Closing Prayer p. 15 in HU

Friday Dark

Breath Prayer p. 140 in MM
Invocation pp. 22–23 in HU
Doxology p. 50 in HU

Opening Verse p. 80 in DM
Night Hymn pp. 88–89 in HU
Antiphon & Night Psalm p. 190 in HM
Antiphon & Night Psalm p. 190 in HM
Psalm Prayer p. 216 in WTW
Litany p. 238 in AE
Closing Prayer p. 107 in DM

Saturday Dawn

Breath Prayer p. 227 in AE
Invocation p. 22 in HU
Doxology p. 13 in WTW
Opening Verse p. 238 in AE
Hymn pp. 72–73 in DM
Antiphon & Psalm p. 231 in HM
Antiphon & Psalm p. 60 in DM
Psalm Prayer p. 240 in AE
Reading p. 50 in TF
Versicle p. 106 in LTF
Responsory p. 267 in AE
Cosmic Canticle pp. 170–171 in SC
Lord's Prayer pp. 56, 58 in HM
Closing Prayer p. 79 in DM

Saturday Day

Breath Prayer p. 261 in MM
Invocation p. 12 in HU
Doxology p. 13 in WTW
Exhortation p. 149 in HU

Antiphon & Psalm pp. 125–126 in TF
Psalm Prayer p. 259 in FM
Meditation p. 212 in HM
Prayer p. 57 in WTW and p. 104 in LT
Lesson p. 43 in HE
Collect p. 42 in HE and p. 32 in AM
Examen p. 44 in HE and p. 273 in AM
Kyrie p. 13 in HU
Benediction p. 199 in MM

Saturday Dusk
Breath Prayer p. 80 in LTF
Invocation p. 18 in HU
Doxology p. 13 in WTW
Opening Verse p. 127 in WTW
Evening Hymn p. 115 in DM
Antiphon & Psalm pp. 128–129 in DM
Antiphon & Psalm pp. 183, 185 in HM
Psalm Prayer p. 59 in DM
Epistle p. 31 in PM
Responsory p. 110 in CE
Cosmic Canticle pp. 117–118 in WTW
Lord's Prayer pp. 56, 58 in HM
Closing Prayer p. 268 in FM

Saturday Dark
Breath Prayer p. 21 in HU
Invocation p. 59 in WTW
Doxology p. 13 in WTW

Opening Verse p. 86 in LLZ
Night Hymn pp. 44–45 in LTF
Antiphon & Night Psalm pp. 75–76 in DM
Antiphon & Night Psalm pp. 76–78 in DM
Psalm Prayer p. 79 in DM
Litany p. 60 in WTW
Closing Prayer p. 148 in HU

Tomorrow Dawn

Breath Prayer p. 101 in LT
Invocation p. 187 in VP and p. 47 in DM
Doxology p. 54 in AE
Opening Verse p. 101 in LT
Hymn p. 187 in VP
Antiphon & Psalm p. 190 in VP
Antiphon & Psalm pp. 137–139 in HM
Psalm Prayer p. 113 in CE
Reading p. 51 in LTF and pp. 65–66 in LLZ
Versicle p. 154 in DM
Responsory p. 56 in DM
Cosmic Canticle p. 184 in CE
Lord's Prayer pp. 56, 58 in HM
Closing Prayer p. 280 in FM

Tomorrow Day

Breath Prayer p. 99 in HU
Invocation p. 179 in SC and p. 66 in LLZ
Doxology p. 54 in AE
Exhortation p. 112 in CE

Antiphon & Psalm pp. 37–38 in CBT
Psalm Prayer p. 61 in AE
Meditation pp. ii, 7 in FM
Prayer pp. 283–284 in WTW
Lesson p. 31 in HE
Collect pp. 125, 165, 168 in FM
Examen p. 101 in LT and p. 313 in AE
Kyrie pp. 234, 236 in MM
Benediction p. 75 in MM

Tomorrow Dusk

Breath Prayer p. 129 in HE
Invocation p. 142 in TF and p. 66 in LLZ
Doxology p. 54 in AE
Opening Verse p. 288 in AE
Evening Hymn p. 81 in WTW
Antiphon & Psalm pp. 73–74 in AE
Antiphon & Psalm pp. 119–120 in TF
Psalm Prayer pp. 86–87 in TF
Epistle pp. 34, 38 in TF and p. 145 in LTF
Responsory p. 240 in CE
Cosmic Canticle pp. 242–243 in WTW
Lord's Prayer pp. 56, 58 in HM
Closing Prayer p. 157 in HU

Tomorrow Dark

Breath Prayer p. 137 in SC
Invocation p. 27 in HM and p. 66 in LLZ
Doxology p. 54 in AE

Opening Verse p. 147 in HE
Night Hymn p. 138 in HU
Antiphon & Night Psalm pp. 224–225 in PM
Antiphon & Night Psalm p. 94 in TF
Psalm Prayer pp. 72–73 in LLZ
Litany pp. 141–142 in WTW
Closing Prayer p. 74 in HU

Teilhard de Chardin

Bibliography and Permissions

We gratefully acknowledge the permissions granted to reproduce the copyrighted material in this book, in particular, agreements made with the Fondation Teilhard de Chardin, the Teilhard estate holders, Georges Borchardt, Inc, and Harper Collins. All rights reserved.

The Divine Milieu by Pierre Teilhard de Chardin. Copyright © 1957 by Editions du Seuil, Paris. English translation copyright © 1960 by Wm. Collins Sons & Co., London, and Harper & Row, Publishers, Inc., New York. Renewed © 1988 by Harper & Row Publishers, Inc. Used by permission of HarperCollins Publishers.

The Letters of Teilhard de Chardin and Lucile Swan. Pennsylvania: Scranton University Press, 2001. Permission granted. All rights reserved.

For distribution rights in the UK and Commonwealth, we

thank Éditions du Seuil for use of *Le phénomène humain*, Pierre Teilhard de Chardin, © Éditions du Seuil, 1955, and *Science et Christ*, Pierre Teilhard de Chardin, © Éditions du Seuil, 1965.

Every effort has been made to trace copyright holders and to obtain their permission for the use of Teilhard's writings. We apologize for any errors or omissions and invite corrections to be incorporated in reprints and future editions of this book.

Summary of Works Quoted in This Volume

Activation of Energy. Translated by René Hague. New York: Harcourt Brace Jovanovich, 1970.

Appearance of Man. Translated by J. M. Cohen. New York: Harper & Row, 1965.

Christianity and Evolution. Translated by René Hague. New York: Harcourt Brace Jovanovich, 1971.

Correspondence: Blondel & Teilhard. Translated by William Whitman. New York: Herder and Herder, 1967.

The Divine Milieu. English translation 1960 by London: Wm. Collins Sons & Co., 1960; New York: Harper & Row Publishers, 1988.

The Future of Man. Translated by Norman Denny. New York: Doubleday, 2004.

The Heart of Matter. Translated by René Hague. New York: Harcourt Brace Jovanovich, 1978.

Human Energy. Translated by J. M. Cohen. New York: Harcourt Brace Jovanovich, 1971.

The Human Phenomenon: A New Edition and Translation of Le Phenomene Humain. Edited by Sarah Appleton-Weber. Eastbourne, UK: Sussex Academic Press, 2003.

Hymn of the Universe. Translated by Gerald Vann. New York: Harper & Row, 1965.

Letters from Egypt: 1905–1908. Translated by Mary Illford. New York: Herder & Herder, 1965.

Letters from a Traveller. Translated by Bernard Wall. New York: Harper & Row, 1962.

The Letters of Teilhard de Chardin and Lucile Swan. Pennsylvania: Scranton University Press, 2001.

Letters to Leontine Zanta. Translated by Bernard Wall. New York: Harper & Row, 1969.

Letters to Two Friends: 1926–1952. New York: New American Library, 1968.

The Making of a Mind: Letters from a Soldier-Priest, 1914–1919. Translated by René Hague. New York: Harper & Row, 1965.

Man's Place in Nature. Translated by René Hague. New York: Harper & Row, 1966.

The Phenomenon of Man. Translated by Bernard Wall. New York: Harper Perennial Modern Thought, 2008.

Science and Christ. Translated by René Hague. New York: Harper & Row, 1968.

Toward the Future. Translated by René Hague. New York: Harcourt, 2002.

Vision of the Past. Translated by J. M. Cohen. New York: Harper & Row, 1966.

Writings in Time of War. Translated by René Hague. New York: Harper & Row, 1968.